To Our Heart's Content
Meditations for Women Turning 50

SuzAnne C. Cole

CB
CONTEMPORARY BOOKS

Library of Congress Cataloging-in-Publication Data

Cole, SuzAnne.
    To our heart's content : meditations for women turning 50 /
SuzAnne C. Cole.
        p.   cm.
    Includes index.
    ISBN 0-8092-3146-8
    1. Middle aged women—United States—Psychology.   2. Middle
aged women—Conduct of life—Meditations.   I. Title.
HQ1059.5.U5C65   1997
305.24'4—dc20   96-44117
                                                        CIP

*This book is dedicated to you,
women turning fifty*

Cover and interior design by Kim Bartko

Copyright © 1997 by SuzAnne C. Cole
Published by Contemporary Books
An imprint of NTC/Contemporary Publishing Company
4255 West Touhy Avenue, Lincolnwood (Chicago), Illinois 60646-1975 U.S.A.
Manufactured in the United States of America
International Standard Book Number: 0-8092-3146-8
15   14   13   12   11   10   9   8   7   6   5   4   3   2   1

Copyright Acknowledgments

Preface

Congratulations on turning fifty! I greet you at the beginning of the second half of your life. As I write this, I'm almost fifty-five, an older sister to you. In my fiftieth year, I began orthodontia, cut my estrogen therapy by three-fourths, lost weight, and started therapy. I began to study my life, plunging into intensive self-examination, extensive reading, and voluminous journaling. I joined women's support groups and discovered the rewards of permitting vulnerability as I shared my stories, thoughts, and emotions.

I'm still learning what it means to be a woman in her fifties in the last decade of the twentieth century, a wife for thirty-three years, mother for twenty-nine, teacher, writer, daughter, sister, niece, mother-in-law, cousin, and friend—among other roles. Daily, I balance conflicting needs—caring for myself while nurturing my family and others; being a friend and good citizen while maintaining my integrity; functioning in the material world while listening to my spiritual self; treating my body kindly without becoming absorbed by it; experiencing nature while living in the city; protecting my solitude while remaining close to those I love; achieving my happiness without hurting others.

Daily I struggle with paradoxes of midlife—to be strong, I must sometimes admit to weakness; to be happy, I cannot avoid grief; to be close, I must sometimes be distant; to be a good companion, I must sometimes be alone; to appreciate brightness, I must accept the darkness that makes it visible; to learn from the past, I must remember without becoming entrapped; to prepare for the future, I must plan for it while living fully and richly in the present.

I want to share my reflections with you through these meditations because I don't think the way I'm experiencing my fifties is unique. On the contrary, it seems to me that when I dare to voice the content of my heart, it is then I find myself most in union with other women.

The quotations that accompany each meditation are by women, not because I haven't been guided, taught, supported, and loved by men, but because *To Our Heart's Content* is woman-centered. I've included titles should you wish to read further in a specific work. The book is meant to be flexible; if the topic for a particular day does not fit your needs, please read one for another day.

Welcome again to your fiftieth year, a jubilee year, a rebirth into the second half of life. Welcome to a plateau where you can sit, reflect on life to your heart's content, and admire the view before setting out for those peaks you see glowing golden in the distance.

Acknowledgments

I could not have written this book without the support, encouragement, teaching, and blessings of others. I am grateful to the women writers I've quoted for their literary grace, common sense, wisdom, and inspiration, and to the C. G. Jung Educational Center of Houston for the programs that introduced me to many of them.

Jane Dystel, my agent, had faith in my idea, taught me how to write a proposal, and sold the book. Susan Schwartz's supportive comments, attention to details, and prompt response made editing and revising practically painless. I also appreciate the careful copyediting of Joan McLaughlin and the efforts of Craig Bolt and Julia Anderson, project editors.

Writers cannot function without constructive feedback; I would like to thank Chris Woods, who teaches as I hope I do; Jeff Lindemann, who supported this book even when it meant abandoning our collaboration; and especially my two writing groups, the Women Writers' Wolfpack—Linda Daigle, Cheryl Peters, Martha Weathers, and Anne Younglove Sadler—and Poetrés—Hallie Moore and Sally Ridgway, who critiqued many of these meditations in draft and were always willing to listen to me read "just one more."

I learned acceptance, honesty, and the value of sharing heart-truths in several women's support groups. And I will forever be indebted to the professionals who have guided my personal growth—Wendy Yelin, who started the process; Holly Miller, who reminds me to breathe and stay in my body; and Jim Matson, who has listened, comforted, confronted, and coached me, helping me reach the truths I've expressed in these meditations.

Thanks to my family—my parents, June and Myrl Chapman, and my sister, Connie Chapman, for always believing I could write; our sons and daughters-in-law, Brad and Elisabeth, Wes and Iulia, and Mike, who have encouraged me to be writer as well as mother; and my husband, Doy, who lovingly gives me the space and solitude I need as well as support and intimacy.

Beginnings

> *"It is easy to see the beginnings of things, and harder to see the ends."*
>
> Joan Didion, "Goodbye to All That"

A new year stretches before us, as pristine as a fresh snowfall. When we were younger, we might have hesitated before so much newness, too concerned with how things might turn out even to get started. But now we know better. So let's go, let's begin this new year, a year in which many of us will turn fifty.

Turning fifty is worth celebrating; we are at last the women we planned to become. Sifting what life has to offer through the fine mesh of wisdom, we have discarded the trash of recriminations, bitterness, and guilt. We cherish what's left—the treasure of good friends and partners, autonomy, serenity. We abandon our concern about endings. Our hearts and spirits rise to greet this new beginning, this first day of the new year.

> *When we start at the beginning, everything else falls into place. I'm thankful today for blank pages, fresh starts, and a renewable spirit.*

Adventure

> *"All children are wild. You lived in the wild*
> *country. Why are you afraid of it?"*
> Ursula K. Le Guin, "Woman/Wilderness"

Our older sisters show us how little aging affects an adventurous spirit. I know a woman who celebrated her ninety-fifth birthday parasailing. My friend Anne, in her sixties, sold her car, rented her house, stored her belongings, and left Texas for a teacher exchange in Hawaii where she knew no one—all this despite a broken kneecap. We women of fifty lead adventuresome lives—learning to scuba dive in the Caribbean, trekking in the Himalayas, walking the Great Wall of China, joining the Peace Corps. Hurrah for us!

When our inner spirits cry out for action and challenge, we respond, buying a backpack or a tent, signing up for ski school, taking a course in sailing, planning a two-week rafting trip. We become as children again, living in wildness.

Say yes to a call to adventure.

Achievement

"If what I do prove well, it won't advance,
They'll say it's stolen, or else it was by
chance."

Anne Bradstreet, "The Prologue"

*A*nne Bradstreet, gifted Puritan poet, mother of eight, addressed these lines in 1650 to the reviewers (mostly male) of her poetry. Even today we may let others take credit for our achievements, or let our fear of failure prevent us from accomplishing tasks and attempting new projects.

We need to erase that fear and claim our achievements—for ourselves and our younger sisters. They should know what older women have accomplished: Maggie Kuhn founded the Gray Panthers after being forced to retire at sixty-five; after a stroke at seventy, Agnes de Mille wrote four books. These women show that success does not happen by chance, but by effort, energy, and labor.

We don't need to trumpet ourselves at the city gates; neither should we hide behind those gates.

Modesty is a virtue; so is recognizing and
honoring our achievements.

Political and Social Activism

> *"I, we all, had such a sense of purpose then. . . . We were forever holding meetings, having endless discussions, arguing, shouting, theorizing."*
>
> Paule Marshall, "Reena"

Those of us turning fifty in the 1990s have had our consciousness raised by the women's movement, we have autonomy, and we enjoy more security than our mothers and grandmothers did. We can challenge what's wrong with the world.

The qualities regarded as quintessentially female—spirituality, nurturing, cooperation, sensitivity to the processes of life—enable us to stand against and change male politics. Our influence can ameliorate dominance, violence, competitiveness, and separateness.

We serve as governors, mayors, legislators, and council members. We elect other women. We work to reform Social Security to reflect women's career and life patterns.

> *"The hand that rocks the cradle rules the world" is a truism. The women's revolution is peaceful and far-reaching.*

Parenting Teenagers

*"I was seventeen, she was fifty. The lines were
drawn, and we did not fail one another."*
Vivian Gornick, *Fierce Attachments*

A state of hostility between parents and teens is typical, no matter the age of the parents. Intimacy with our children seems to disappear when they are in mid- and late adolescence—by their choice. Living with teenagers presents challenges at any parental age, but we have more time and resources to deal with them than younger parents do. Because we also have experienced transitions and crises, we can better understand and empathize with their painful alterations. We can divest ourselves of ego involvement in their struggles and wait patiently for them to tell us what they need. We know the child who slams the door in our face today will pour out his or her heart tomorrow. We can wait.

*If I have forgotten what I was like as an
adolescent, somebody in my family probably
will be happy to remind me.*

Being Authentic

*"She was becoming herself and daily casting
aside that fictitious self which we assume like
a garment with which to appear before the
world."*

Kate Chopin, *The Awakening*

The freedom to be truthful, to live instinctively, to pursue tasks and jobs that give us joy is a gift of being women in our fifties. It's as though all the roles we have played before have prepared us for now. Altering or discarding inappropriate roles, we let our true selves dominate the parts we play rather than letting the roles become our real selves.

Finally free from reacting to the criticism of others, we develop our inborn talents and attributes. We may sing a solo in public for the first time, let our hair go natural, or dump our overly critical "friends" or our dead-end jobs.

All our lives, we've been preparing for now; we are finally the women we dreamed of becoming.

I know now that I can't be anyone but myself.

Bitterness

"There is a time in our lives, usually in midlife, when a woman has to make a decision . . . about whether to be bitter or not."

Clarissa Pinkola Estés,
Women Who Run with the Wolves

We all have reason to be bitter. We should have been named chairwoman of the charity drive—but we weren't. Our mother should have given us the Eastlake bedroom suite—but she left it to our sister. Our friends' adult sons invite them on vacations—but ours didn't. No wonder we feel resentful. Life simply hasn't turned out the way we expected; we haven't received what we deserved.

We can't choose what happens to us, but we can choose how we react. Will we refuse to work for the charity or will we serve it in another position? Will we quit speaking to our mother or congratulate our sister on the bedroom suite? Will we ignore our son or invite him to go on a holiday with us? It's our choice.

Bitterness sours life; I'd rather savor the sweetness.

Death

> *"But of course, death may be just what one
> has been waiting for; it may explain
> everything."*
>
> Rebecca West, "Parthenope"

*W*omen have an extraordinary ability to face death, the darkness that from time to time overshadows all life. We need this strength now. We are statistically more likely to lose our parents when we are between the ages of fifty and sixty than at any other age. We may lose partners and friends, and we will also consider our own mortality. When we confront these losses—potential and actual—with courage, we gain wisdom. If we cling to the illusion there is no death, we think we have forever to live the lives we really want to live. Accepting death frees us to live fully. Surviving deaths that cause major changes in our lives helps us realize that in survival itself lies hope for the metamorphosis of grief into joy.

*When I accept physical death as part of the
human condition, I gain perspective and
strength.*

Dieting

"Dieting with fierce will-power is the masculine route; dieting with love of her own nature is the feminine."

Marion Woodman,
The Owl Was a Baker's Daughter

*I*s there a woman who's never dieted? In high school, we may have worn girdles to make us svelte. When we had babies in the 1960s and 1970s, some obstetricians told us not to gain more than twenty pounds, so we may have dieted in pregnancy. When we were thirty and forty, we tried fad diets, exercise, and willpower, and we dropped a few pounds . . . for a while.

But somewhere in midlife most of us came to terms with the bodies heredity has given us. We care for them more gently, treating food as the nourisher of life rather than its enemy. We try to eat contemplatively and appreciatively and find we don't need to eat as much as we used to eat. We learn the difference between physical hunger and emotional hunger.

There is a place in my life for chocolate-chip cookies and carrots.

Turning Fifty

> *"The year I became fifty felt like a great*
> *coming together for me. I was very proud of*
> *having made it . . . in my own style. 'Time*
> *for a change,' I thought. . . ."*
>
> Audre Lord, *A Burst of Light*

At fifty, we stand firmly at the midpoint of our lives, looking backward and forward. We are proud of what we have accomplished, and relinquish what we always suspected we couldn't do anyway—managing the lives of others. Instead, we grasp firmly and kindly the only person over whom we legitimately exercise power—ourselves.

We see ourselves as stable and centered, no longer fragmented by the multiple duties and responsibilities and roles of younger years. We face the future with enthusiasm, vigor, and relish. Being born within us on this momentous birthday is a new self. We feel capable, optimistic, and courageous.

> *I am fifty. I know who I am and what I want.*
> *My fears are behind me and my future is full*
> *of promise.*

Friendship

*"Each friend represents a world in us, a world
possibly not born until they arrive. . . ."*

Anaïs Nin, *Diary*, Vol. 2

*O*ne of the riches of being midlife women is the ripening and maturing of our long-standing friendships as we realize, perhaps for the first time, how much we depend on the support and help of our friends. We can be totally honest with them because they've shared our triumphs—the birth of a child after ten years of trying, unexpectedly swift promotions in a "male" field, an art exhibit at the local library—and our tragedies—another cross-country move, illness, a child's failed marriage. They know what we need, often before we do. They bring out unexpected talents and capabilities by believing in us. They reflect us and protect us. They listen compassionately, never mentioning they've heard the stories before. Sometimes they tell us what to do; sometimes they lovingly wait through the darkness with us in silence.

*Time invested in friendship is time invested in
my best self. I will call a friend today.*

Initiation

> *"With age comes a new initiation, this one*
> *reflective, . . . deepened by the insights of*
> *experience."*

Starhawk, *Spiral Dance*

*W*e read of rites of passage into adulthood involving isolation, privation, and scarification followed by celebrations. And we may think of being initiated into the meaning of life, of awakening to full consciousness of ourselves, as a task of adolescence. However, initiations precipitated by major life-changes and necessitating spiritual rebirth, also occur in midlife. Once wives, we now may be divorcées or widows; once mothers, now grandmothers or great-grandmothers; once executives, now retirees.

We may initially postpone or flee awakenings because of pain, the almost inevitable companion of initiation. Yet we remember that in pain lies possibility. Without pain the caterpillar does not metamorphose into the butterfly. Without pain we cannot give up addictions. Without pain we cannot remember and learn from the past.

> *I can choose to accept initiation into my real*
> *self no matter what my age.*

Joy

"Why, why do we feel
(we all feel) this sweet
sensation of joy?"

Elizabeth Bishop, "The Moose"

*I*n this poem the sight of a female moose standing in the middle of a road dissolves the grit and tension of daily life and seizes the watchers with joy. For us, joy may spring from sighting the first violet blooming in the woods, or watching small children at a petting zoo, or sitting silently in a darkened theater watching a great actress perform.

Joy takes us out of ourselves to something beyond ourselves, something felt rather than learned. And, as in the poem, joy often springs from something shared, a *we* rather than a *me* experience. In joy we intuitively know ourselves to be part of a holy whole, witnesses to the sacred. Individual concerns fade as we become aware of godliness within and without. We are nothing and yet we are everything. Logic vanishes, reason disappears. Joy is.

I will let myself be surprised by joy.

Loneliness

> "And the loneliness in her life, the emptiness,
> was filled with a steadiness and grace for
> necessary things."
>
> Estela Portillo Trambley, "The Burning"

*M*ost of us will spend some time in our lives alone. If we have children, almost half of our adult lives will be spent without children at home and almost a quarter of our lives with neither children nor a husband. Yet Jungian analyst and author Jean Shinoda Bolen has said that often the happiest women she meets in her lectures and travels are women in their sixties and seventies who live alone.

Choosing not to be lonely if alone, some of us return to our first mother, Nature. Hiking in the Appalachians in a soft spring rain, eating a bagel in the park during a work break, or watching cardinals and blue jays squabble at a backyard feeder reminds us that we, too, have a place in the grand design of the world.

Loneliness need not be terminal; the cure is in my hands.

Menopause

> *"Menopause is the gateway into the most
> sacred time of a woman's existence on earth,
> a time when she can at last discover the
> deeper meanings she has sought."*
>
> Lynn V. Andrews,
> *Woman at the Edge of Two Worlds*

*M*enopause is the most obvious physical manifestation of turning fifty. Its symptoms—hot flashes, night sweats, insomnia, vaginal dryness, weight fluctuations, and mood swings—become familiar. The change of life energizes some of us, incapacitates some, and hardly touches others. We can help each other through menopause by neither minimizing nor exaggerating our experience.

And we can remember its benefits. In her audiotape *Wise-Woman Archetype*, Jean Shinoda Bolen says the blood we once retained in our bodies to make children now makes wisdom. She recommends marking the onset of menopause with ceremony and ritual as an initiation into the stage of being a wise-woman.

> *Menopause is one of the hallmarks of being a
> woman; both the onset and the cessation of
> menses are cause for celebration.*

The Past

"Like the I Ching *says, returning to one's roots is returning to one's destiny."*
Sandra Cisneros, *"Bien* Pretty"

The past provides the bonds that hold us to places and people; remembering the past connects us to ourselves. Climbing with friends on their country property one spring, I was suddenly seized by greed. I wanted their property to be mine—the hills, the pretty creek, the wildflowers. Confused by my envy and ashamed of it, I said nothing; thinking about it much later, I realized the overwhelming desire had risen from my past.

As a child I loved spending summer vacations on my grandparents' Kansas farm. Running free through fields and barns, I assumed everything I saw belonged to me. For a few moments during that afternoon with our friends, I had been the favored child of summer again, proud possessor of all I surveyed.

Because the past is always with me, I can recognize and befriend it.

Growth

*"The only continuity possible in life as in love,
is in growth, in fluidity—in freedom. . . ."*
Anne Morrow Lindbergh, *Gift from the Sea*

Occasionally, we become restless, vaguely dissatisfied, irritable, even mildly depressed without knowing why. Lindbergh suggests these moods, so typical of adolescence, also may be signs of midlife growth and change. Although at times we must sit awhile with despair and stagnation, and even tolerate regression, in general, the pattern of our life is toward fluidity rather than fixity, toward growth rather than stasis. Few of us wish to remain the same at all costs; all of us know such permanence is impossible. Once we have gathered what our souls require from an experience, a job, or a relationship, we will move on, growing until we die.

Growth is painful, but I will not resist it.

Power

> *"Having information, expertise, or skill in manipulating objects is not the primary measure of power for most women. Rather, they feel their power enhanced if they can be of help."*
>
> Deborah Tannen, *You Just Don't Understand*

As we move into the twenty-first century, many of us believe that the differences in the way women experience and utilize power will be the salvation of the world. Because women are more interested in conflict resolution than in war, we need to move our voices from the bedroom to the boardroom and from notes on the refrigerator door to legal briefs.

If we have been subject to male authority for large parts of our life, we know what it is like to be out of touch with our own power. And that knowledge gives us a different perspective on power. Knowing that power can corrupt, when we acquire power, we can share it. Instead of power *over*, we can seek power *with*.

Women exercise power by empowering others.

Serenity

*"Make one's center of life inside of one's self,
not selfishly or excludingly, but with a kind of
unassailable serenity. . . ."*

Edith Wharton, *A Backward Glance*

"*S*erenity" would be a beautiful name for a woman, a woman sitting peacefully, empty hands cupped comfortably in her lap, face relaxed, lips curved in a faint smile. Complete in herself, lacking nothing, needing nothing from anyone else.

We, too, can seek serenity anytime we wish. Here and now, we can breathe into our bellies as we envision a place of comfort. Dining alone, we can forget the frustrations of the day and concentrate on the perfect pairing of food and appetite. Stuck in traffic, we can let go of our irritation and be grateful for a moment when we can do nothing else but be with ourselves.

*Serenity comes when, wherever I am, I center
myself and trust myself.*

Meaning

> *"Each thing and every moment derives a
> meaning from a context one is meant to
> understand."*
>
> Marianne Wiggins, *John Dollar*

*I*f we've been searching for meaning all our lives, now we may feel we have found it. Now we use our wisdom, experience, and intuition to understand why different events occur, why some relationships go well and others don't, why we sometimes act as we do. We can make meaning from our life events because we have the context of experience and reading and shared knowledge. No longer flung about like a tiny boat on a storm-tossed lake, we have rudders, compasses, oars, and anchors. So outfitted, we can survive the storms of life and return safely to port, understanding what has happened and learning from it.

> *I make my own meaning, test it with my
> experience, and hold it aloft as a guiding
> beacon.*

Sexuality

"Yes, I, an old woman, a grandmother many
times over—I hunger and burn! And for
whom? For an old man. And having said
that, I feel like throwing my hands before my
face and laughing out loud. . . ."

Ruth Prawer Jhabvala,
"The Man with the Dog"

ecent studies effectively expose the lie of a marked decline in sexual activity in midlife. Sexuality continues, largely unabated, to the end of life; sexual rediscovery and sexual freedom form part of the pleasure of life after fifty.

Sexuality plays such an important role in who we consider ourselves to be that it mustn't—and needn't—be neglected. We have the leisure to devote to sexual exploration, a wealth of experience to enhance it, and the knowledge that the pleasure of the process is as much fun as the goal of orgasm. No longer concerned about sexual attraction as a lure for reproduction, we can explore a full range of sexual pleasure.

I am now, as I have always been, a sexual
being.

Simplifying Our Lives

> *"How easy it was to strip things away. To discover that once you took the pictures curtains rugs and flowerpots, you were still there. None of it bound you."*
>
> Jean Thompson, "Driving to Oregon"

Something in us begins to respond to the call of simplicity at midlife. Maybe it's dusting souvenirs and wondering why we once found the snake carved from a coconut such a charming piece of folk art. Maybe it's scanning our stacks of unread books and realizing that not only have we not read this year's bestsellers, we haven't read last year's either. Maybe it's trying to stuff another bargain blazer into an already overcrowded closet.

The appeal of possessions, so strong a desire at one time in our lives, wanes. Paring down our lives can begin with discarding something old when we bring home something new. For each new outfit—one outdated ensemble to the thrift shop. A new painting that captures our imagination—a painting we're tired of to the charity auction.

Today I will simplify my life by giving away one unnecessary item.

Solitude

"There is a strength in solitude."

Vera Cleaver,
"If It Is Not Good, Make It So"

*I*n our demanding, noisy, clashing world, we yearn for solitude, but sometimes we hesitate to claim it. We may fear being thought inordinately selfish for retreating into solitude. Or we may fear the solitude itself, the emptiness stretching before us with no distractions and nothing planned.

For me, the hardest part of a period of solitude is beginning it. I regularly take one-day retreats, confining myself to one room of my house (except for bathroom and very short meal breaks), and allowing myself no activities except journaling—no music, no reading, no exercise. The first hour or two of withdrawal is always the worst. Mild claustrophobia hits me as I close the door on myself, often followed by overwhelming grief. I submit, it passes, and slowly I adjust to solitude. Later, I leave my retreat refreshed, renewed, clearheaded, and clear-eyed.

I can find my strength in solitude.

Walking

"Did you know that walking for ten minutes has a more measurable calming effect than a Valium?"

Linda Bamber,

"The Time-to-Teach-Jane-Eyre-Again Blues"

*W*hat do walkers see strolling through the seasons? Rosebuds swelling with promise, a pair of squirrels playing tag in a live oak tree, a padded and helmeted five-year-old wobbling on in-line skates, a new house being swaddled and stapled in foil insulation.

The repetitive motion of putting one foot in front of another, making steady progress, soothes us; progress in other areas of our lives often cannot be observed. As our bodies move, our thoughts flow unimpeded and unceasingly, so unlike their stumbling and halting when we're physically inactive.

Walking and talking with a partner can be a much better method for problem solving than sitting and talking. Silence while sitting may be construed as estrangement; silence while walking is companionable.

Grateful for a body that moves, today I'll take a walk.

Change

> *"Only a person who has experienced, accepted,*
> *and acted the entire human condition—the*
> *essential quality of which is Change—can*
> *fairly represent humanity."*
>
> Ursula K. Le Guin, 'The Space Crone"

$\int$ ometimes we neither want nor expect change, but it happens anyway, so we've learned not to fear it. In fact, we've experienced change in so many ways that we've learned to accept it. Our bodies constantly change as cells die and slough off to be replaced by other cells. Our dreams and expectations have changed—we no longer want what we wanted when we were twenty-five or forty-five or last year—or even yesterday—and sometimes that's good.

We balance within us a tendency to resist change, to surround ourselves with the comfort of the familiar and safe and the impulse to see change as good, to be pioneers in the process of change, eager to discover and work with what's new.

> *Of course, not all change is for the best—but I*
> *will do my best to make it so.*

Work

*"When an activity is in harmony with oneself
it requires less energy and effort."*

Jane Hollister Wheelwright,
For Women Growing Older

*W*ork is not work when we enjoy it, or as Jungian analyst Jane Wheelwright says, when it is in harmony with ourselves. Although we struggle against this wisdom, instinctively we know it. "Oh, all right," we mutter between clenched teeth, agreeing to take on a job we don't want, a responsibility suiting neither our interests nor our talents. Immediately the task becomes Herculean. We get tired just thinking about it. But dutifully we plow on even though we find it tedious and enervating. Nothing is at hand when we need it; nothing just falls into place.

When will we learn? We have many talents, but we can't do everything, and sometimes we just don't like some jobs. Why not make other choices when we can?

*I don't have to batter my way through work;
like water, I can flow around it and reach the
sea just the same.*

Practicing Art

> *"Whether making art is your career or your hobby or your dream, it is not too late or too egotistical or too selfish or too silly to work on your creativity."*
>
> Julia Cameron, *The Artist's Way*

ow is a good time to reacquaint ourselves with the creative little girls we were, who laid out houses of stones and twigs, exuberantly splashed brilliant watercolors across white butcher paper, and told stories to a circle of friends.

Now is a good time to practice art. We may find ourselves to be skilled artists, but we don't have to be to find pleasure in creating. We don't have to let anyone, including ourselves, judge our creations, because we recognize the value of the process. Art transforms life, allowing us to see, for example, how painful experiences often produce wisdom. Art helps us understand ourselves and others; we don't create art to be great artists but to be greater women.

> *When I birth the artist within me, I give myself generosity, joy, understanding, and courage.*

Pessimism

> "A Blemish player is someone who has mastered the art of seeing a flaw in everything. . . . It's a guaranteed system for feeling disappointed."
>
> Rita Justice, *Alive and Well*

essimism is probably more innate than learned. Some people seem to have been born pessimistic and cannot free themselves from their prisons. We avoid those who flee felicity because we fear being enveloped in their gloom. We also tire of supporting pseudopessimists, those whose insecurity solicits our denials: "My proposal won't be accepted." (*Please say it will be*.) "I'll never look as good as you do." (*Please say I do*.)

Pessimism warps reality. After all, it doesn't rain every day, even in Seattle. Yes, we may be cheated, but not daily. Yes, sometimes misfortune strikes, but seldom is it permanent.

I'd rather expect to become a butterfly than live in a perpetual cocoon of pessimism.

Sorrow

"They say sorrow chastens, I don't believe it;
it hardens, embitters. . . ."

George Egerton [Mary Chavelita Dunne],
"Virgin Soil"

By now, most of us have experienced sufficient sorrow. Sorrow can harden and embitter, yet few of us seem so shriveled by our sorrows to be incapable of ever again feeling happiness. In pain, once we open ourselves to receive kindness, we begin to heal. We learn that if we bear our sorrow with honesty and courage, it will eventually recede. If we have felt ourselves superior to others or apart from them, sorrow chastens us by reminding us of our common humanity. We can turn sorrow into a gift of restoration and renewal by weeping for others as well as for ourselves. Then sorrow confers peace and calm and joy rather than adding to the anger and hatred of the world.

I have known sorrow and I have known
sunshine; experiencing darkness helps me
appreciate daylight.

Progress

"People tend to think that life really does progress for everyone . . . but actually only some people progress."

Alice Walker, quoted in Claudia Tate, Ed.,
Black Women Writers at Work

*P*rogress has a duality that sometimes makes us uncomfortable. On the one hand, living fully implies movement, flowing streams rather than stagnant ponds. We've progressed in education, careers, relationships, maturity. We understand the necessity of progress, and we approve of many of its products—frozen foods and microwaves, live transmissions of symphonies and concerts, e-mail, credit cards, antibiotics, smallpox and polio vaccines.

But when we see charming vine-clad brick bungalows bulldozed and replaced by sterile apartment blocks, when majestic oaks are leveled for parking lots, we're not so certain all progress is good. And we may wonder if, in our own progress, we have bulldozed or severed some of our valuable parts. We want to move forward, but not at the expense of others or ourselves.

I will evaluate progress—mine and my community's—regularly.

Assertiveness

> *"If women growing older have the spunk, they*
> *will look about for . . . what is personally*
> *satisfying to them."*
>
> Jane Hollister Wheelwright,
> *For Women Growing Older*

We need to assert our rights as human beings, caring for ourselves and our needs, saying no, and remaining loyal to our friends and our convictions. Assertiveness is not aggression; assertiveness is following our curiosity, risking ourselves, expressing a drive for life. Assertiveness doesn't mean telling others what they are doing wrong because it focuses on self rather than others. Assertiveness replaces *you* statements—"You shouldn't spend so much time playing golf"—with *I* statements—"I'm lonely when you play golf every weekend."

We may face opposition when we assert ourselves for the first time or when we move to a more forceful level of assertiveness, but we must stick it out. In time others will accept the new us.

> *I will stand up for myself, stating what I believe*
> *and what I need and how I want it.*

Careers

"To love what you do and feel that it
matters—how could anything be more fun?"
Katharine Graham, *Ms.*, October 1974

Turning fifty provides an excellent vantage point from which to look back on our careers, evaluate the choices we've made, and decide what changes we would like to make. Fifty is not too late to start another career; serial careers offer solutions to burnout and professions that change rapidly.

When we no longer feel passion for what we do, when we no longer feel that our work matters, perhaps we should consider different fields for our skills. We want to be able to say more at the end of the day than simply "I'm still here." We want to feel energized when engaged in our jobs, cheerful at the end of the day, satisfied with what we have accomplished. We want to realize there is nothing we would rather be doing.

My career is my lifework; I will work at my life.

The Future

> *"There are years that ask questions and years that answer."*
>
> Zora Neale Hurston,
> *Their Eyes Were Watching God*

We have no guarantee on our future, but because we've lived comfortably to fifty, the odds are good that we have many more years to live, maybe even another fifty. Yet few of us expect the second halves of our lives to be like the first, nor would we want them to be.

In our first fifty years we've been busy doing—getting an education, finding partners, creating families, rearing children, establishing ourselves in careers and professions. Humming with energy, running, restless, striving, questioning. Now we've reached a plateau, begun to level out, stabilize, slow down, relax, look around and enjoy the view, listen to the answers, move into *being* rather than *doing*. We reorganize our priorities. We confront the fact of our eventual death, and we begin to focus on the years we have left to live.

I don't know what will happen in the future, but I welcome it with joy.

Dreams

*"The dreaming mind may be compared to a
movie director, picking up things from waking
life that need more attention than we have
given them. . . ."*

Ann Faraday, *The Dream Game*

*W*hen we fall asleep, the curtain rises
on a rich, complex dreamworld with
characters, plots, dialogue, and themes from the daytime
world so rearranged and transformed that it sometimes is
unrecognizable.

We choose how we react to dreams, whether or not to
work with them, and how to interpret them. When we
dream, for example, of driving a car backward with no
brakes at a high rate of speed, we may check our actual
brakes. Or we may believe the dream indicates negative feelings about our current life paths or a profound lack of control over some major area of our life. Which interpretation
is correct? Because dreams are as unique as our finger-
prints, the interpretation that resonates for us is the correct one—for us.

*I will value my dreams because they illuminate
my life.*

Pain

"That long, blind, doorless and windowless corridor of pain was waiting to open up and shut her in again."

Sylvia Plath, *The Bell Jar*

*W*e may find that as we age, pain becomes more bearable because it grows more familiar. We can sense how long it may last, we may know what causes it, and we have learned when to struggle against it and when to submit. We also have learned to name our pain rather than lie to ourselves about its causes.

Without minimizing the terrors of physical and emotional pain, pain also has positive aspects. It sensitizes us to repressed feelings that, once released, find expression in creativity. Pain teaches us about our bodies and spirits, helping us recognize hostile forces and negative influences. Pain cleanses us like a powerful tidal wave, sweeping away petty irritations, minor confusions, and small resentments. When pain passes, we are left empty and purified—and grateful for small pleasures.

Pain comes as part of life. I can endure its embrace.

Mothering Young Children

*"Sometimes the strength of motherhood is
greater than natural laws."*
Barbara Kingsolver, "Islands on the Moon"

*M*any of us choose to become mothers at later ages. A woman of fifty profiled on the evening news had just given birth to triplets and anticipated no unusual problems in rearing her children. Diane Keaton at fifty adopted a baby girl. Men of sixty, seventy, and even eighty father children without criticism—often, in fact, with admiration and respect.

If we embrace motherhood now—again or for the first time—we bring the wisdom of midlife to the experience. We're less nervous, more relaxed, and easier on ourselves and our young children. We have more financial security. We're more secure in our accomplishments, so we're better able to relax in our careers and leave sixty-hour weeks to others. After all, what do young children need the most? Love, shelter, nourishment, security, stability. Who better to provide these gifts than us?

Motherhood is not a quality of age but of the heart.

Crisis

> *"Immersed in a situation like this you throw*
> *overboard everything . . . that's not*
> *meaningful or essential for survival."*
> Isabel Allende quoted in Cathleen Rountree,
> *On Women Turning Fifty*

The dangers we face in crisis situations are being overwhelmed, becoming immobilized or panicked, attacking ourselves for our presumed inadequacies, or continuing to use familiar methods even when they fail. When we realize that old responses no longer work, then we can try to resolve the crisis.

The key to living with and through crisis is judging what must go, stripping down to the essentials, conserving energy for the struggle. Thus crisis can be a purifier and an equalizer, purging the extraneous, reducing life to its most important aspects. We've learned to weather crisis by creating peace within ourselves to withstand the storm outside. We may not always win in each crisis, but we gain in the struggle a sense of our own strength.

> *I can float through the rapids of a crisis rather*
> *than battering myself against the rocks.*

Becoming a Crone

"The crone can afford to be honest. . . . She is
free. Who she is cannot be taken from her."
Marion Woodman, *Leaving My Father's House*

"*C*rone" is a traditional, venerable term for an older woman. We're not crones yet, but we will be; now is a good time to think about who we want to be when we are. We choose as mentors for our cronedom older women we admire, women who impress us with their vigor, vitality, purpose, and single-mindedness. The passion of these wise-women may be directed toward serving the greater community. Or their adventures may be personal and private—they may be grandmothers who sense their immortality and connectedness through their grand-children and through loving a few, expanding that love out-ward to others. We choose women who concentrate on a few important things, stay close to nature, get involved in something outside their own homes, and have many friends of many ages.

I will become a crone-in-training by looking for
a mentor and developing my passions.

Feminism

*"To allow oneself at fifty the expression of
one's feminism is an experience for which
there is no male counterpart. . . ."*
Carolyn G. Heilbrun, *Writing a Woman's Life*

$\mathcal{F}$eminism is the belief that women are entitled to full participation and leadership in all human activities from intellectual to spiritual, social to sexual. All of us who believe women are fully human are feminists. Even if we have never particularly felt our gender to be an obstacle to anything we wanted to do or be, it is difficult to be female and not to be feminists. And the vast majority of us believe feminism has improved women's lives.

Feminists battle sexism wherever we find it, even within our own hearts, for feminism begins with ourselves, understanding ourselves and what we want, then broadening to encompass other women because we want them to have what we have. Whatever we do as strong women contributes to feminism.

*I am female; I want my sisters to be accepted
as fully human; I am a feminist.*

Depression

> *"So sometimes one has simply to endure a
> period of depression for what it may hold of
> illumination if one can live through it,
> attentive to what it exposes or demands."*
>
> May Sarton, *Journal of a Solitude*

Twice as many women as men suffer from depression, a state of unabated melancholy in which we anticipate nothing and weep without reason. No wonder we seek release from this doleful prison. Yet depression has its values. It forces us into self-examination to find what's missing in our lives or what we are tolerating that suffocates our core beliefs. Like the canary in the coal mine, depression warns of something toxic close at hand.

If our depression is gray rather than totally black, perhaps we can wait it out, courageously examining our lives, listening to its lessons, and taking our inner selves as our authorities. We can remember that depression often is a passive form of rebellion against outer authorities who force us into unsuitable patterns.

*Depression provides an opportunity for
introspection.*

Domesticity

> *"If this domestic life were so very good, would*
> *your young men wander away from it, your*
> *maidens think of something else?"*
>
> Florence Nightingale, *Cassandra*

*M*y German great-grandmother Christine reportedly stopped one day while rolling out dough to ask, "Be I making cookies or be I making pie?" I hurry upstairs to grab the clothes out of the dryer before they wrinkle, stop to answer the telephone, walk back downstairs to check my calendar, remember I haven't defrosted anything for dinner yet, dig out a package of chops, notice we're out of milk, start a grocery list, and then, two hours later, climbing the stairs, I remember the clothes. Pie dough or cookies? Who knows? Who cares?

Even when we take pleasure in domestic duties such as setting a lovely table, arranging a vase of flowers, or polishing silver, our pleasure often fades when we realize how ephemeral that work is.

> *There are times when I enjoy being domestic,*
> *and there are times when I'm glad to have other*
> *work.*

Feelings

"Her feelings aren't right. Really good people
have the right kind of feelings deep inside;
then the rest takes care of itself."

Jane Augustine, "Secretive"

*T*oo often we shut off or repress our feelings for fear that they "aren't right"; others won't approve. We need to observe the expressiveness of young children, to notice how spontaneous and intense their joys and sorrows, their anger and fears. They don't "know" enough yet to deny or censor their feelings.

Acknowledging and expressing our deepest feelings may be temporarily painful as we realize how afraid we are to lose our youthful beauty or how much we hate an officious colleague. Emotions may drag us back to the past to confront and grieve childhood trauma too long repressed. Because emotional repression can cause physical illness, however, expressing our feelings brings us health and ultimately liberates us.

I will value and respect all my feelings, the ones
I like and the ones I don't.

Memories

"If you remember something, then it's true. . . . In the long run, that's what you've got."

Barbara Kingsolver, *Animal Dreams*

Our memories need not always be verifiable to be valid. We can argue with a sister for years about whether the toy we once fought so bitterly over was Barbie the bride or Barbie the beauty queen and never know for sure. What we do know, what we remember, is the intensity of the struggle, the sorrow we felt when our struggle scalped the doll, and the resolve that grew, unbidden and unconscious, to protect our potential children from such sadness. Those feelings constitute the truth of the memory.

For us, what's important about memories is not their factual fidelity, but the emotions associated with them, like the fragrance lingering in a room after a bowl of hyacinths has been removed. We don't reject memories because others doubt the details; we know what effect they had on us.

I trust my memories.

Duty

"She felt no desire to shrink from duty, . . .
but she sighed for some comforting assurance
of what was duty."

Elizabeth Stuart Phelps,
"The Angel Over the Right Shoulder"

*D*utifully we met our obligations; ironing sheets, baking cookies and
bread, working late night after night, volunteering for half-
a-dozen charities, scrubbing the house every Saturday,
keeping current with all correspondence.

And yet as hard as we worked, our duties didn't seem to
make us joyful. We frowned at our work. Duty was our stern
taskmaster; we had to be dutiful even when it strangled us.
We reminded ourselves of children being taught "to do their
duty" in the toilet; this kind of self-righteous, cheerless
duty was rubbish. So we redefined duty to include our duty
to ourselves, our health, and wholeness. We decided to perform the jobs we enjoyed and share, delegate, or drop the
others.

Duty strangles; deeds performed out of love
liberate.

44

Love

"I love thee to the level of everyday's
Most quiet need, by sun and candlelight."
Elizabeth Barrett Browning,
Sonnets from the Portuguese

In midlife love acquires new meaning as we relax into relationships grown strong and sturdy through the years, relationships both tender and dependable. For us love is supportive and caring, kind and selfless, patient rather than possessive. In love we expect sharing, touching, pleasure, but we no longer expect love to be perfect, nor do we hold it to some impossible ideal.

Instead, we expect intimacy as well as intercourse; we no longer are afraid to open ourselves completely to the one we trust and love, to be naked, body and soul, with another human being. Experiencing union, our boundaries dissolve.

We can extend love because we have it to give, and receive love because we consider ourselves worthy of it. We love our partners and spouses for who they are, just as we expect to be accepted.

Love lasts.

Nature

*"I was walking in the woods and became
aware suddenly . . . of a deeply peaceful
kinship with all that is alive. . . ."*
    Susan Griffin, "Thoughts on Writing"

Women and nature, a link as ancient and respected as time itself. Mother Earth, Mother Nature, Gaia, Terra Mater—by whatever name we know her, we acknowledge and value that connection. In nature we experience a mystical union with creation and accept her reality—hurricanes and humming-birds, warthogs and spotted fawns, cockleburs and orchids, sandstorms and summer dawns. Perceiving our kinship with all of creation helps us accept and love every particle of ourselves as part of that creation, nothing ignored, dismissed, or shoved aside. Nature never tries to be what it is not. When we acknowledge our own nature with similar equanimity, we experience our power.

*May I never forget to honor my first mother, the
Earth.*

Dying

> *"Things were finished somehow when the time*
> *came; thank God there was always a little*
> *margin over for peace. . . ."*

Katherine Anne Porter,
"The Jilting of Granny Weatherall"

*F*acing the death of the body is our final initiation into wisdom. When our future has a name and perhaps even a date, we can cease worrying about it and concentrate on what we consider most important. As Alice James, dying of breast cancer, wrote in her diary, "one revolves with equal content within the narrowing circle." Because we narrow our focus, dying enables us to live fully in our remaining time. And, as we have tried to model how to live for those we love, so now we model how to face death with wisdom and courage. When the dying we watch is not our own, we remember that when we truly love, we can be willing to let the other go first.

> *I cannot choose how or when I will die, but I*
> *can choose to live my remaining life fully.*

Grace

> *"Experiencing the present purely is being emptied and hollow; you catch grace as a man fills his cup under a waterfall."*
>
> Annie Dillard, *Pilgrim at Tinker Creek*

When we offer cheerful kindness and friendship to those who need it even when they don't deserve it, we practice grace. We recognize grace when we meet it operating through others who comfort and strengthen us. My women's support groups allow me to experience grace as recipient, giver, and witness. When one of us speaks from a heart full of pain while others listen without judging, silently offering expressions that speak, "I know, I understand, you are not alone," grace suffuses the room.

Life gives us the opportunity to practice grace daily—to let another driver in ahead of us, to smile at the cashier who gives us the wrong change, to forgive the friend who lets us down.

May I always be able to extend and receive grace.

Losses

> *"The art of losing isn't hard to master."*
> Elizabeth Bishop, "One Art"

*A*ll losses are not equal. When we talk about loss, we may be talking about positive losses—five pounds, negative and bitter acquaintances, feelings of inadequacy. When we give up what no longer helps us, loss forces us to try something else, to move into the unknown, to take some risks. And there's something very promising about that.

Or we may be thinking of more hurtful losses—the promotion we didn't get, friends who moved away, relatives who died. Yet we know we cannot protect ourselves from loss. We cannot hold on to anything forever—neither cherished possessions nor youthful figures nor friends and relatives—and perhaps we shouldn't. Perhaps we need to think about mastering the "art of losing."

> *I cannot prevent loss, but I can prevent myself from overreacting to loss.*

Perfection

*"Susan looked untouchable, clean, as if she
had attained a kind of solitary perfection that
she had always been aiming for."*

Jane Smiley, *Duplicate Keys*

A father talks to his small son who's berating himself over his karate performance. "So, Alex," the father says, "you want to be perfect. Who's perfect?" The boy responds, "God and the angels [long pause] . . . and dead people."

Exactly. Alex at seven seems to have grasped something many of us still struggle with. Perfection is an impossible goal, one achieved only by the supernatural—and the dead. Yet how hard we try to be perfect in relationships, perfect at work, perfect at home. Daily we toil, grimly gritting our teeth, straining against immovable barriers. Along the way, we lose a sense of humor, perspective, and juiciness. We alienate partners and colleagues. We raise our blood pressure and ulcerate our stomachs and colons. For what? Terrible, frozen, deadly perfection. Is it worth it?

*To be imperfect is to be human and alive. I will
allow myself to be imperfect.*

Ritual

*"One of the great tools of the weavers of
culture is ritual. . . . Ritual is the way culture
enacts and affirms its values."*

Starhawk, *Truth or Dare*

*W*omen have always marked rites of
passage—birth, puberty, marriage,
childbirth, death—with rituals that center our communities. Ritual affects our behavior by affecting our minds;
events marked with ritual acquire significance. Ritual also
works with mystical forces to affect material reality, evoking the supernatural presence we so often sense during
ceremonies.

Through ritual, essential ideas become embodied in the
symbolism of exchanging rings, blessing food, exchanging
kisses of peace, placing stones on graves. Because ritual
frames the present in the past, each time we participate, we
experience the ceremony on another level. Yet not all rituals are permanent; many arise spontaneously in response to
needs, and when we no longer need them, they vanish. Ritual implies an attitude of sacred wonder; rote behavior is
habit rather than ritual.

*I will honor the important events of my life with
ceremony.*

Pets

> *"Thank God for sending me an animal soul, so patient and understanding, never using its tongue to harass or harm me."*
>
> Zhang Jie, "An Unfinished Record"

y Maltese, Squirt, is in his seventeenth year. He's friendly with the rest of the family and guests, but he's my dog; I'm the one he shadows from room to room and greets at the door with undemanding, forgiving, uncritical affection.

Squirt reminds me to live in the present. He doesn't mourn the days when he could jog three miles with me and almost catch a teasing squirrel or a trespassing cat. He doesn't torture himself with memories of being attacked in his own yard by a dog who slashed open his belly. He's happy with today—fresh water and kibble, a spoonful of cereal when I breakfast, a biscuit after he gets brushed, a patch of sunlight, low windows to view the world from, a little conversation, and some petting.

Loving my pet makes me more human.

Praise and Flattery

*"Sweet words are like honey: a little may
refresh, but too much gluts the stomach."*

Anne Bradstreet,
Meditations Divine and Moral

*T*he ability to praise sincerely when praise is due is difficult for some of us. We know when to praise the Creator, when to praise the awesome and the exceptional, but sometimes we find it difficult to praise the people in our daily lives. Perhaps we feel ourselves too bound by the cords of jealousy to applaud. Perhaps we think praising someone else denigrates ourselves.

Or perhaps we overdo praise to the point of flattery. Genuine praise restores, rebuilds, affirms, and validates; flattery sickens. Genuine praise reinforces self-esteem, while flattery bases itself on false premises, "too much sugar for a dime" as the saying goes. We do not flatter to pander, to win the approval or affection of others. We do not have to flatter those we love; we praise them.

Help me to avoid flattery and deserve praise.

Relationships

> *"A truly loving, liberated relationship is*
> *healthy, life-affirming, mutually beneficial and*
> *empowering to both parties."*
>
> Pearl Cleage, *Mad at Miles*

We long for relationships. Deep within us lies a need to be with others with whom we can be totally honest and with whom we can speak of the deepest things of our heart, knowing our words will be accepted and respected and never used against us.

When we have such relationships, we nurture and preserve them by maintaining our respect for each other, by performing kindnesses and small courtesies, by realizing that relationships change and develop, and by allowing each other to be separate as well as part of a couple. Concentrating on relationships to the neglect of self is detrimental.

If we yearn for such a relationship, we can work at living with ourselves as well as with others. We can seek companionship while keeping our self-esteem, sense of proportion, and sense of humor.

> *I will treasure, protect, and maintain my*
> *relationships.*

Aging Positively

"*To become a fully grown woman . . . in Native American Tradition happens around the age of fifty-two. . . .*"
   Jamie Sams, *The 13 Original Clan Mothers*

So at fifty, we're not even fully grown yet. We're just coming into our own, and there's no stopping us now. Perhaps we've known that all along. We know we've been growing braver as we grow older. We care less about what others think. We worry less. We've become our own authorities. We take more risks. We attempt more ambitious projects. We feel freer to do what we want to do. We dare disapproval.

We liked ourselves at forty-nine and we will like ourselves at fifty and fifty-five and sixty. We know that each year of growth adds another level of depth and richness to our souls, wisdom to our minds, and compassion to our hearts.

I enjoyed my youth and I'm ready to be a grown woman now.

Ambition

> *"I came into a group of marvelous individuals*
> *who had lots of healthy aggression. It was*
> *okay to be ambitious. We cheered each*
> *other on."*

> Jane Kenyon, *From Room to Room*

For some of us, pleased with our accomplishments, midlife may be a time to let go of ambition, settle into our careers, become more supple and flexible and less goal-oriented. But others may just now be permitting ourselves the first sparks of ambition, the desire to be more, want more, do more. Perhaps we've just achieved freedom from taking care of others. Perhaps we've carried the ambitions of others for too long, and now we're free to use our energy to pursue personal goals. Perhaps we've just figured out what we want to do with the rest of our lives, or we've finally found a task that has inflamed us with passion. For us, it's time to own our ambition.

It's up to me whether my ambition becomes a
vice or a virtue.

Tenderness

*"To think that the possibility of such
tenderness exists and we don't use it all the
time. . . ."*

Ellen Gilchrist, *Starcarbon*

What a saving grace is tenderness, the softest form of kindness, and in how many different ways we see it manifested. A small child squatting in the straw of a petting zoo, holding softly between her hands the muzzle of a small goat. An old Scottie, her body curved tenderly and protectively around the head of a toddler, sound asleep in a cocoon of blankets. The gentle hands of a woman bathing her mother, confined to bed with a broken hip. A student in my writing class critiquing a peer's weak paper—"You made me think about that differently."

We must not be afraid to reveal our tenderness, to crack our armor just a bit and free our softness. Otherwise, the armor may rust shut. Then where would we be?

*I will try a little tenderness today—beginning
with myself.*

Psychotherapy

*"Asking for help does not mean that we are
weak or incompetent. It usually indicates an
advanced level of honesty and intelligence."*

Anne Wilson Schaef,
Meditations For Women Who Do Too Much

If we're timid about seeking help from
therapists, it helps to remember that
almost everyone can benefit from the self-examination that
therapy fosters. Those of us who are or have been in therapy have discovered just how much the therapeutic process
can contribute to our growth and transformation.

It's also good to remember that it's never too late to
benefit from therapy. Therapy at our age can set into
motion changes that have been a long time coming. It can
help us crystallize decisions that have been hovering form-
less and vague just below our conscious awareness. Therapy
respects our processes; therapists provide guidance while
letting us make the decisions.

*If I need professional help and guidance, I will
never consider myself too old to seek it.*

Illness

> *"Illness is the night-side of life. . . . Everyone who is born holds dual citizenship, in the kingdom of the well and in the kingdom of the sick."*
>
> Susan Sontag, *Illness as Metaphor*

To be human means suffering occasional illnesses—the flu, periodic migraines, seasonal allergies, or more oppressive afflictions. Yet, as difficult as it may be to realize at the time, illness has gifts. In illness we must slow down, rest, and treat ourselves with kindness and respect, something many of us find difficult without that excuse. Illness forces us to rely on others—medical professionals to heal us and colleagues, friends, and partners to take over some of our daily responsibilities. Learning to trust others in our vulnerability is good for our souls.

Despite physical illness we can continue to be mentally, spiritually, and emotionally healthy—curious about the world and grateful for its pleasures.

I don't choose illness, but I can choose to accept its gifts.

Anger

"A curse from the depths of womanhood
Is very salt, and bitter, and good."

Elizabeth Barrett Browning,
"A Curse for a Nation"

So many events elicit our anger. A cashier refuses to admit ringing up the wrong price. A housepainter passes off an inferior paint as the equal of the quality product we paid for. The city library, suffering a cutback in funding, closes two days a week. Our ex–son-in-law refuses to pay child support.

We feel heat rising from our bellies. We want to explode. But our internal censors admonish us: "It's not nice for women to get angry, dear. Think about what you will look like. What will people think?" We choke back our words, swallow our rage, clench our teeth, and put on our smiling masks. We need to remember that anger signals something wrong, not with us, but with our environment. Righteous anger purges and cleanses.

Expressing anger can be good for me—and my world.

Beauty

"I think we are all capable of tremendous
beauty once we decide we are beautiful. . . ."
Nikki Giovanni, *Gemini*

Watching a production of *Follies*, I was struck by the beauty of the joyful, kicking, strutting chorus line whose average age was well above sixty. Their beauty reflected wisdom, compassion, cheer, energy, confidence, and power; they had earned it. They didn't give a hoot in hell for their wrinkles and softly rounded bellies—and neither did we.

We have no need to mourn the beauty titles of our youth because the beauties of midlife are equally impressive. We know our bodies, we know what becomes us, we know how to use cosmetics and dress advantageously if we choose to. Some of us prefer facing the world honestly and naturally—no hair coloring, no makeup, no uncomfortable clothes chosen for fashion alone. And we too are beautiful.

I am beautiful because I am unique; there is
only one me.

Inner Child

*"Who is the child of our future development
who we somehow lost, abandoned or never
knew in earlier life?"*

Jean Prétat, *Coming to Age*

*W*e can reclaim the children we once were, giving ourselves now the blissful childhood we may have missed then. We can delight in liberating our inner children from their dark prisons barred with "can'ts" and "don'ts" to frolic and play in the sunlight of adult freedom. For when we free our inner children, we free ourselves. Haven't we all observed the untroubled face of a child effacing the lines and frowns of age in a truly happy adult? So when someone says or implies we're too old to do something, we say "baloney." Then we feel the tiny little girl we carry inside jump with joy as we go right ahead and roll down that inviting soft green hill, say yes to a midnight swim, or walk barefoot in squishy mud.

*I reclaim and cherish my inner child as my
past — and my future.*

Conscious Living

"Perhaps it is better to wake up after all, even to suffer, rather than remain a dupe to illusions all one's life."

Kate Chopin, *The Awakening*

wakening to our full potential as human beings often occurs in midlife. Sometimes awakening has pleasant results as dormant abilities and talents such as needlework, sketching, a facility for languages, or solitary traveling are aroused. And sometimes awakening is painful when we realize we don't like to cook the holiday feasts the family expects, we quit soul-deadening jobs even though others depend on us, and we end relationships that no longer permit us to be ourselves.

Although others might prefer that we remain "sleeping beauties," dozing uncomplainingly through the passage of time, waiting for princes to wake us with magical kisses and tell us who we are and what we should do, we can awaken ourselves. We can leave a note telling the princes where to find us.

I choose not to sleepwalk through life.

Self-Confidence

"In the past several years, I have learned, in short, to trust myself."

Erica Jong, "Blood and Guts: The Tricky Problem of Being a Woman Writer in the Late 20th Century"

*A*cting from self-confidence can be problematical, even in midlife, if we confuse self-confidence with arrogance or self-importance or even insolence. But self-confidence is none of these. It is knowing what we know—being assured, secure, calm in the face of chaos and crisis, feeling self-sufficient, realizing we have all the understanding we need.

Self-confidence walks proud, needing neither to be propped up nor to trample over. When we are self-confident, we respect ourselves and our sisters and speak up for what we want and need with no apologies. We believe in our ability to make decisions and manage our environments. We've been there and done that; we know how. We know what we like; we won't accept less. We are what we are, and we won't change to please anyone but ourselves.

If I think I can do it, I can.

Empty Nest

> "She knew . . . what happened to women of
> fifty at the height of their energy and ability,
> with grown-up children who no longer needed
> their full devotion."
>
> Doris Lessing, "To Room 19"

$\int$ helves above my computer hold Russian lacquer boxes, Zuni fetishes, a pottery angel holding a rabbit—and a small bird's nest collected one winter on a long country walk with our sons and daughters-in-law. Looking at it reminds me of our warm companionship that chilly day as we walked and chatted.

It also reminds me of the empty-nest syndrome that, despite the claims of sociologists, many of us do not suffer. With children no longer demanding our attention and talents, we turn our fullness toward developing long-neglected parts of ourselves. We're relieved to be no longer responsible for stuffing gaping beaks. We relish our children's independence and enjoy relating to them as dear adult friends.

Having an empty nest does not mean
emptiness. My life is full of possibilities.

The Soul

"The soul is silent.
If it speaks at all
it speaks in dreams."

Louise Glück, "Child Crying Out"

I dreamed once we had been conquered by benevolent "overlords" because we had become too aggressive and materialistic. Although others seemed happy about the transition, I was grief-stricken. Assembling to be given a new identity, I stuffed a pillowcase with my journal, some photo albums, and two ornate Victorian brass candlesticks. One of the overlords gave me several identity cards and indicated we would change roles frequently because nothing, including my sorrow, was ever permanent. My only constant, my only possession, was my soul. "Everything else," she said, eyeing the pillowcase, "must be discarded."

Misery overwhelmed me as I asked, "What of my children, my grandchildren-to-be?" She answered gently, "They were never *your* children; they belong only to themselves. But all the world's children are yours." I realized in that dream the truth many of us accept at midlife—no one and no thing belongs to me except myself.

Only my soul is permanent.

Femininity

*"When she stopped conforming to the
conventional picture of femininity, she finally
began to enjoy being a woman."*

Betty Friedan, *The Feminine Mystique*

When we equate femininity with passivity, weakness, dependency, trivial concerns, and irrationality, we proclaim ourselves unfeminine. Living up to those cultural standards of femininity produces female impersonators and stifles women's souls. Yet if femininity means possessing attributes such as giving, nurturing, connecting with others, expressing feelings, and being vulnerable with those we trust, we neither want, nor do we need, to give it up.

We also explore our masculine side, developing such "masculine" attributes as independence, assertion, finding fulfillment in careers, and pride in physical prowess and strength. In the end, we integrate masculine and feminine qualities because emphasizing one to the exclusion of the other leaves us only half a person.

*To be fully human is to be aware of and use all
my strengths — both feminine and masculine.*

Goals

> *"Surely life must be more than something just*
> *to be practically and sensibly got through?"*
> Fay Weldon, "In the Great War"

*S*etting and maintaining realistic goals gives meaning to our lives. Shopping for the holidays wearies us, but the goal of pleasing those we love makes the tiredness worthwhile. Goal-oriented tasks such as learning a language, mastering tai chi, or simplifying our lives relieve anomie and depression.

However, when we consistently find ourselves failing to meet our goals, we should analyze them. Maybe we apply the standards of others to ourselves, so our goals are not truly ours. Maybe we state goals negatively rather than positively. Maybe we've outgrown our goals; for example, personal growth and self-fulfillment may suit us more now than career-oriented goals. As we change and grow, our goals should develop along with us. Otherwise they recede into infinity and become unattainable.

A goal is a plan, not a proscription.

Hypocrisy

*"Tomorrow, she'll be genuinely warm and
accepting. For tonight, hypocrisy will have
to do."*

Margaret Atwood *The Robber Bride*

Sometimes, our hunger for affection and approval motivates actions and words that betray our integrity. We compliment when we should condemn and flaunt behaviors in public we don't actually practice in private.

To cure ourselves, we learn to recognize the feelings of discomfort engendered by hypocrisy, the faint uneasiness that spoils our pleasure in the approval for which we trade integrity. We begin to realize our inner guardians will let us know when we are wrong if we sensitize ourselves to their presence. Then we work hard at being honest in all aspects of our life, forgoing the hypocritical word or deed and risking dislike and disapproval.

*Practicing hypocrisy denies and denigrates my
values. I will practice integrity instead.*

Making Lists

> *"Alison Stockman . . . went through, for*
> *perhaps the fourteenth time, her List. She*
> *was not a natural list-maker . . . ."*
>
> Rosamunde Pilcher,
> "An Evening to Remember"

Some of us *are* "natural list-makers," beginning innocently enough with requests for Santa, progressing to listing school assignments, the names of our friends' pets, and birth dates to remember. Lists help us organize our lives, but sometimes list-making gets out of hand and begins to control our lives. We may find we can't say yes to anything without first checking a list. We may be unable to depend on our memory because we don't use it. We may make endless lists of minutia. And we may beat ourselves up for being unable to cross off enough items on our lists.

When making lists makes us feel worse about ourselves rather than better, when our lists become mandates rather than guides, then we may want to reconsider their value. Perhaps we have become addicted to the "listing" rather than the "making."

> *If I think my life will end if I lose my list, then*
> *I probably need to moderate my list-making.*

70

Women's Rights

> *"Women don't get half as much rights as they*
> *ought to; we want more, and we will have it."*
>
> Sojourner Truth,
> "What Time of Night It Is"

Sojourner Truth, freed slave, abolition-
ist, fervent supporter of women's
rights, spoke these words in 1851. Unfortunately the conditions she protested still exist. Women provide most of the
unpaid work in this country from housework to caring for
aged parents and grandchildren. We lack sufficient safe,
affordable, quality child-care facilities. In most professions,
women still receive less salary than men do in equivalent
jobs. Violent crimes against women, including rape and
domestic violence, continue to increase.

Women's rights—to have our unpaid work valued; to
earn equal pay; to control and make decisions about our
sexuality and reproduction, free from coercion and violence;
to education; to political power—are really human rights
that should, as a matter of course, be extended to all.

Working to extend the rights I enjoy to every
other woman is my responsibility.

Plans

> *"If you want to make God laugh, tell her your plans."*
>
> Anne Lamott, *Bird by Bird*

nne Lamott reminds us that "life," as someone has said, "is what happens when we're making plans." Leading useful lives requires some planning. But we needn't be as tied to our plans as Precious Pearl to the railroad track. We need enough slack to roll free when that express locomotive, life, comes barreling down the track. When someone offers dinner out, we don't refuse because we planned to cook a stir-fry meal. We put the vegetables back in the crisper and go gleefully out the door.

Plans can be tucked away in a desk drawer just as Jane Austin used to put away her novels when life interrupted her writing. Happiness in planning requires flexibility, certainty that our plans do not depend too much on others for their fulfillment, and avoiding the mistake of postponing living while waiting for our plans to come to fruition.

> *I can plan without becoming a servant to my plans.*

Spontaneity

> *"The more I learned to follow my impulses in a*
> *playful way with colors and forms, the weaker*
> *became my allegiance to conventions of an*
> *aesthetic or any other nature."*
>
> Alice Miller, *The Drama of the Gifted Child*

Spontaneity responds naturally, joyfully, and playfully to events, without being constrained internally or externally. Truly free women live spontaneously because we trust our inner selves as true guides. We decide whether expressing our spontaneous thoughts or doing what we want at this very moment is indulgent or if it will nourish us; if it will, then we speak or act.

Spontaneity can't be scheduled. We have to recognize and seize the moment—for giving a hug, dancing alone to a favorite tune, or hopping in the back of a pickup for a ride through the autumn mountains.

> *When I remember the joy of being a*
> *spontaneous child, I am willing to risk being*
> *impulsive.*

Money

*"When you are in control of your money, you
are in control of your life."*

Elinor Lenz, *Rights of Passage*

Our salaries are no longer a matter of secondary importance for most of us. More than half of all working women now provide 50 percent or more of our families' financial support. We take pride in supporting ourselves and others and in being successful in real jobs. Because money often defines power and value in our society, we happily define ourselves in part by our income.

Yet in midlife we may also find ourselves restructuring our lives, choosing work that may not be rewarded by money, giving up the pursuit of power that may have dominated us earlier. We may want to work for ourselves without considering whether or not we will make money. Money may become less important as an indicator of happiness in a job than meaningfulness. And that's fine, too.

*Money is essential to happiness, but only I can
determine how much money I need.*

Obligation

> "What if a woman allowed herself to leave a
> mode of doing that does not nourish her, that
> actively makes her unhappy?"
>
> Judith Duerk, *Circle of Stones*

We recognize that our activities have become obligations rather than fulfillment when we don't want to get up in the morning because we feel no joy in the coming day. At day's end, we sigh with dissatisfaction. Our accomplishments nourish our souls no more than cotton candy nourishes our bodies—a momentary sweet taste of achievement followed by emptiness.

When we feel this way, we probably need to give up some of our labor, which may disappoint others. But if our work doesn't feed us, if we work from obligation rather than from our hearts, we would do well to quit. There's always other work to be done and other opportunities more suitable for our needs and our talents.

When we recognize the source of our
unhappiness as our doing, we can do something
about it.

Spirituality

> *"It is the bread of art and the water of my*
> *spiritual life that remind me always to reach*
> *for what is highest within my capacities and*
> *in my demands of myself and others."*
>
> Audre Lord, *A Burst of Light*

*T*he spirituality that manifests itself in us is not pale, ethereal, otherworldly; it's warm, rich, nourishing, earthy, even political. Our spirituality manifests itself inwardly as we connect with our inner selves and outwardly as we honor our connection with all living forms.

Organized religion, mystical revelation, relationships with others, art, and nature may all feed and develop our spirituality. These spiritual wellsprings help us face down our fears of aging and death because we realize these mysteries are not the question. The question is whether or not we have the courage to be who we are, spiritual as well as material beings.

> *Today I rely on my spirituality to help me*
> *bring light to the world rather than darkness.*

Day-to-Day Living

*"Our task is say a holy yes to the real things
of our life as they exist. . . ."*
Natalie Goldberg, *Writing Down the Bones*

Sometimes we need to remind ourselves of the pleasures of our ordinary "real" life. We want to appreciate an ordinary day, a day in which "nothing" happens except . . . we awaken rested, someone who loves us greets us with a smile, the morning paper lies at the door, the car starts, meetings have purpose and end on time, lunch tastes good, the radio station plays our favorite melody, we fall asleep easily at bedtime.

An ordinary day—yet how wonderful the reality, the events, and the people we take for granted. How wonderful to create order, whether in a sock drawer or in a squabbling office. How wonderful to make a good job of whatever we have been given to do, sweeping a kitchen or planting a forest. How wonderful to be surrounded by people who keep commitments. How we would miss these elements of an ordinary day if they were taken from us.

*I will cherish ordinary days as extraordinary
gifts.*

Waiting

*"If only he'd sent out scouts, if only he'd
waited! But waiting can also be fatal."*
Margaret Atwood, *The Robber Bride*

*W*omen are well accustomed to waiting. We wait for weather to change,
telephones to ring, letters to arrive. We wait for the children
to graduate from high school before we go back to school.
We wait for our husband's next promotion before we treat
ourselves to a holiday. We wait until we've finished the
dishes, folded the laundry, and cleaned up the den before
we sit down to capture an image for a poem. We wait and
we wait.

Rushing can be distracting and even dangerous, but waiting can also be destructive. While we wait for the children's
graduation, the course we wanted closes for lack of enrollment. Our husband's next promotion never comes. When
we sit down to write the poem at last, it has vanished.

*There is a time for waiting and a time for
doing; I will decide which is which.*

Process

> *"Feminine consciousness is concerned with*
> *process. It sees the goal as the journey itself*
> *and recognizes that the goal is consciousness*
> *of the journey."*
>
> Marion Woodman, *The Pregnant Virgin*

*W*omen concentrate on process because so many of our tasks have unattainable or indiscernible goals; child rearing, for example, is a process that never reaches completion. Our sons and daughters will always be our children—and we will always be their mothers.

We become fully involved in the processes that engage us. Rather than hurrying along, pushing and pulling toward *the goal*, we savor the process itself. We're like the Tibetan Buddhist monks and nuns who take days to construct intricate mandalas of colored sand. However, when they finish the design, they scrape it away, discarding the sand in the nearest stream. The process of making the mandalas is the act of worship—not the finished designs.

I find as much pleasure in doing as in
finishing.

Telling Our Stories

"The longing to tell one's story and the process of telling is symbolically a gesture of longing to recover the past. . . ."

: bell hooks, *Talking Back*

Telling our stories helps us make sense of what happens to us. As Isak Dinesen once said, "all sorrows can be borne if you put them into a story or tell a story about them." We experience release when we permit support groups, trusted friends, partners, and therapists to hear our stories.

Sometimes we don't even realize how something made us feel until we hear ourselves describing it. As we talk, struggling to describe an event or conflict, we begin to make something of the story, seeing our actions more clearly, perhaps understanding we had no other choices.

If our listeners are sympathetic and wise and can offer the observations we want, that's fine. But we may not even need their comments. Sometimes the most important thing is simply that we have told and they have listened.

My stories are my truth; I will tell them.

Spring

*"Spring . . . doesn't unfurl in slow, sweet
ribbons. It comes in with ruffles and
flourishes, a whoop of rowdy azaleas,
battalions of tulips, a cannonade of dogwood."*
Anne Rivers Siddons, "Spring in Atlanta"

*A*nne Rivers Siddons captures the drama of spring. Spring arrives in a blare of trumpets with marching-band frenzy—colors clashing, raucous birds strutting their territories, squirrels dashing through trees in delirious mating frenzy. There's an element of extravagant excess about spring and an endearing, gawky, coltish awkwardness.

There's foolishness in spring, a holy foolishness. We need its green juiciness racing through our veins, causing us to walk barefoot in the mud until our toes cramp, garden far too long on the first mild days, dance crazy dances with children. Celebrating because we've made it through another winter; we're leaving the hearths of winter and emerging from caves and cellars into the fresh pale sunlight of spring.

*Spring, province of the newborn and the reborn,
was made for me.*

Stress

> *"The natural response to stress and crisis is not breakdown and capitulation, but transformation and renewal."*
>
> Toni Cade Bambara, quoted in
> Ann Charters, Ed.,
> *The Story and Its Writer* (4th Ed.)

*Q*uarrels with a partner, missed credit-card payments, news of a child's impending divorce—our muscles tighten, fists clench, guts churn, and breathing becomes rapid and shallow. Stress warns us of attack; our bodies prepare to fight or flee. Repressing this energy may cause high blood pressure, migraines, spastic colons, or panic attacks.

Trying to nurture the world also causes stress. We must become aware of how we react to stressors and learn to control our reactions through stress reduction—meditation, prayer, self-hypnosis, deep relaxation, music. We can pay attention to our needs, desires, and hopes. And knowing we can't live with chronic stress, we can try to eliminate its causes.

> *Stress is a normal response to an abnormal situation. I will try to remove causes of stress from my life.*

Appearance

*"I don't wear the right clothes in the closet or
explain how I am me
I come as I go translucent oh what you get is
what you see"*

Jean Valentine,
"The Free Abandonment Blues"

On days when I write at home I wear comfortable pants with elastic waistbands, baggy shirts, and sheepskin moccasins. No makeup. No jewelry. When I go out, sometimes I wear makeup, fashionable outfits, pretty jewelry—and sometimes I don't. Dressing up is fun when I choose it. It wouldn't be pleasurable if I felt I had to look good to keep a man or attract one; it wouldn't be fun if it consumed most of my time and energy.

Dressing to please ourselves is a freedom of our age, as we sometimes take great care with what we wear, and sometimes we don't bother. Sometimes we like calling attention to our womanhood; some days we don't. We're long past the point of confusing who we are with what we wear.

Dressing to please myself makes me happy.

Solitude

*"She wanted the depraved luxury of solitude
and quiet in which she would be restored
(enriched, oh yes! . . .) to the familiar limits
of her own being."*

Nadine Gordimer, "Comrades"

*W*omen often have difficulty establishing and justifying our need for
solitude because we're so well trained in putting others'
needs before our own. Yet if we cannot replenish our own
springs by periodically retreating into solitude, how can we
expect to quench the thirst of others?

Solitude nourishes us, renewing our active selves when
we're exhausted by constant contact with and service to
others. Solitude strengthens us, quiets the mental chatter
that jangles our nerves, and restores our creativity.

We can create solitude for ourselves by unplugging
phones and letting answering machines take calls. We can
hang "do not disturb" signs on our study, office, and bedroom doors—and mean it. Then we can pray and meditate
and work—alone.

*Solitude is coming home to myself; I will seek
solitude today.*

Menopause

> *"The climacteric is a time of stock-taking, of*
> *spiritual as well as physical change, and it*
> *would be a pity to be unconscious of it."*
>
> Germaine Greer, *The Change*

*S*ome of us miss natural menopause. At forty-two, recovering without complications from a total hysterectomy, I found myself one post-surgical morning inexplicably weeping. "It's hormones," said my male surgeon, putting me on a high dose of estrogen, and that was that. No more symptoms, no more menopause. Except that for years afterward, I dreamed of wandering endlessly through vast deserted buildings, fruitlessly seeking the babies whose cries echoed everywhere, and awaking to find my breasts and heart aching.

Denied a conscious, natural passage into the world of wise-women, we can redeem that loss if we choose. I have reduced my estrogen dosage and am tolerating some of menopause's physical symptoms to reexperience it chronologically, physiologically, and psychologically.

Menopause deserves attention; I will be
conscious of mine.

The Future

> *"I don't know what will happen in the*
> *future. . . . Right now I am free floating."*
> Michele Murray,
> "Creating Oneself from Scratch"

*N*o, we don't know what will happen in the future, but we know what it feels like to live in it now. We don't have to think so much about consequences. So we may decide not to wait any longer to . . . dump the disagreeable friends, study the subjects we always wanted to instead of the useful, practical ones we did, travel to Greenland, live abroad, or sell the suburban house and move to a loft apartment downtown.

Self-understanding is the most important piece of luggage we can carry into the future. It's time to listen to and honor all the parts of our personalities. We need to reflect on where we've been, plan where we want to go, and make any necessary adjustments.

> *My future belongs to me; I will choose the best*
> *equipment for the trip.*

Anxiety

"Without anxiety life would have very little savor."

May Sarton,
The House by the Sea: A Journal

When we suffer anxiety over even joyful events—job promotions, vacations, weddings, foreign travel—it's good to remember that anxiety can lend "savor" to our lives. We also can realize that anxiety is neither abnormal nor terminal. Anxiety prepares us for situations by reminding us that we've faced something similar before. Mild anxiety reflects a wish to do well and can even help us perform.

If anxiety paralyzes us, however, we can lessen its effects by planning ahead for all contingencies If our anxiety seems bound to the past, we can work with our anxious memories in full and deal with them as mature women. Experiencing anxiety can toughen us, making us spiritually and emotionally stronger.

I will not be anxious about situations out of my control; I will use my anxiety about other events to help me prepare for them.

Health

"The self-care necessary to be well begins with self-value. Deciding on wellness reflects and fosters that self-value."

Marilyn Bentov *et al.*,
The New Ourselves, Growing Older

Those of us who reach fifty with neither heart disease nor cancer have a good statistical chance of living to be ninety-plus. The quality of our lives from now on depends in part on physical health. We owe it to ourselves to get enough exercise and rest, eat properly, avoid or eliminate stress, and become aware of and control our addictions.

It's also our responsibility to demand good medical care. Studies show that the shortest doctor visits are those between a female patient and a male doctor—and the longest are those between a female patient and a female doctor. We want physicians who provide timely information and view the doctor/patient relationship as a partnership.

My health is my responsibility; I will take charge of my body.

Possessions

> *"I grow upset, angry, depressed beyond all*
> *measure at the amount of time and effort we*
> *give to mutable things."*
>
> Michele Murray,
> "Creating Oneself from Scratch"

Instead of wanting to acquire more "stuff" now, we may find ourselves wishing to get rid of things as we realize the effort involved in itemizing, insuring, cleaning, repairing, waxing, protecting, watering, positioning, and illuminating our possessions.

There's nothing wrong with enjoying pretty things or with wanting to be comfortable, but how many things do we need? Sometimes we wonder if we wouldn't really be happier with a cabin and a mattress, a toilet, a few books, and some paper and pens. Yet when we start listing what we'd eliminate from our lives, we find good reason for keeping almost everything. Perhaps all we can do is be mindful when we buy more stuff.

> *I don't mind owning things as long as they*
> *don't own me.*

Autonomy

> *"The God of woman is autonomy."*
> Alice Walker, *Possessing the Secret of Joy*

utonomy means seeing ourselves connected to others by shared values, love, friendship, and familial ties, but also separate from them. Autonomy means stating our differences—and allowing others to do likewise. Autonomy means affirming our beliefs—and validating them with our behavior. Autonomy means making choices—and adhering to them.

At some point we all stand alone; it is essential, then, to know where we stand in the universe as human beings and to recognize the nature of our relationships with others and with ourselves. A T-shirt slogan reads, "Behind every successful woman is herself." The helping hand we seek often can be found at the end of our own arm.

> *I am autonomous; I am not an extension of*
> *anyone else, nor do I require someone else*
> *telling me what to do.*

Being Single

> *"The older I have grown, the more serious and*
> *irremediable have seemed to me the evils and*
> *disadvantages of married life, as it exists*
> *among us at this time. . . ."*
>
> Harriet Martineau, *Autobiography*, Vol. 1

*R*ecent studies prove that single women enjoy better social lives and are healthier, mentally and physically, than single men. Women living alone do not live in isolation, nor do we live without psychological and social support. We maintain close and loving ties with family and friends. If we have no children, we find other children to guide, listen to, and love.

We often fulfill our lives and ambitions more easily than women who are part of a couple, perhaps because maintaining relationships takes so much time and attention. (And living alone is certainly preferable to being isolated in an unloving relationship.) Being alone provides time to grow, achieve clarity, and figure out what we want for ourselves without considering the needs and wants of a partner.

Living alone does not mean being alone.

Foolishness

> *"I proclaimed that Laughing Out Loud is the*
> *Virtue of Crackpot Crones who know we have*
> *Nothing to lose."*
>
> Mary Daly, *Outercourse*

No longer so caught up in how we appear to others, we don't mind "playing the fool" sometimes as part of learning. At fifty-one, on skis for the first time, I fell down trying to navigate from the rental shop to the school. Bound by crossed skis, I had no idea how to get up. A Japanese gentleman bowed and politely, formally, helped me to my feet. I thanked him graciously, essayed one step, and fell again. With ceremonious propriety, he pulled me upright; I managed three shuffles before falling again. This time he hoisted me up and pushed me from behind all the way to the school. I looked ridiculous . . . but I began to learn to ski that day.

Sometimes playing the fool is the height of wisdom.

Clarity

*"There is, for me, something immediate—a
path, a lantern, that either passes for clarity
or else gives me the patience or the willingness
to make my way through the underbrush."*

Ellen Bryant Voigt, "On Tone"

After hours or days of tangling ourselves in knots or tracing one thought only to find it disappearing into another, clarity flashes through our misconceptions with the startling brilliance of lightning. We make ourselves receptive to clarity by taking the time we need to study confusing situations. By meditating and praying. By laying out our dilemmas to sympathetic listeners who ask the right questions and offer to restate what they hear us saying.

We also know that clarity sometimes reveals what we'd rather not do. Even though we asked for it, we may not want to put into action drastic changes or surrenders. But achieving clarity doesn't mean having to act on it; we may simply be thankful for its arrival.

Clarity dazzles, but it doesn't have to blind.

Empowerment

> *"Empowerment of women will come when we identify with women older than we are and not before."*
>
> Baba Copper, quoted in Jo Alexander *et al.*, *Women and Aging*

*A*ll women need to be empowered, not just our age group and our younger sisters, daughters, and granddaughters, but our mothers and older sisters as well, the women we will become. To be meaningful, gains achieved in business, marketplace, legislatures, and educational institutions must be extended to all women.

We can become politically active and we can educate ourselves about the needs of aging women. We can spend time with older women, crones who have much to teach us and deep, rich life experiences to share. Every age has its own developmental tasks; we prepare for our own old age by associating with older women. Any achievements we obtain through empowering them will empower us as well.

It is in my own best interests to work for the empowerment of older women.

Privilege

"To acknowledge privilege is the first step in making it available for wider use."
Audre Lord, *A Burst of Light*

Sometimes as women we feel part of such an underclass that we can't consider ourselves privileged. But our black and brown sisters tell us we're privileged if we're white. Our homeless sisters tell us we're privileged if we have shelter. Our battered sisters tell us we're privileged if we've never been abused. Our sisters working for less than minimum wage tell us we're privileged if we have financially secure jobs with some benefits.

To be unaware of our blessings because we take them for granted or because they seem insignificant to us in light of the greater gifts of others is dangerous. Our privilege is a blessing and a resource; using it for political and social good requires awareness.

I will take advantage of my position of privilege.

Shame

"What shames us, what we most fear to tell, does not set us apart from others; it binds us together if only we can take the risk to speak it."

Starhawk, *Truth or Dare*

Few of us are immune from the insidious voice of shame because as children we were made to feel ashamed about natural curiosities, explorations, and perhaps even our need for love and attention. When we innocently told the truth about family secrets, we were attacked and silenced—and made to feel shame. Thus the reactions of others can still easily make us ashamed of ourselves—not just of our liabilities and deficiencies but even of our creativity and talents.

As Starhawk suggests, the cure for shame is to acknowledge and own it. When we feel safe enough to expose our shame to daylight, we may find that what we feared as something setting us apart from others, a gargoyle on our forehead, is, instead, a decorative detail we share.

Shame can cripple; the cure is to love myself.

Fantasies

> *"The acceptance of a new challenge in middle*
> *or old age marks the end of fantasy, and the*
> *substitution . . . of work."*
>
> Carolyn G. Heilbrun, *Writing a Woman's Life*

*D*o women fantasize too much? Does daydreaming waste time and weaken our willpower and resolve? If we continually fantasize about the same improbable occurrences, then perhaps we do need to analyze our illusions to discover their causes. Maybe they indicate something in our real world that requires immediate action. Fantasies should not replace reality or work, nor should we hold on to the same unattainable fantasies forever. However, we can use them to modify reality, making it more palatable and more endurable. We can fantasize what we want and who we want to be, especially when we have no mentors or real-life models to follow. Fantasies can lay out plans and make goals more attractive, cloaking them with romance and magic and "what ifs."

Fantasies are chocolate for my mind—a treat
but not a steady diet.

Support Groups

> *"I am aware, however, that the support of women has changed my life."*
>
> Natalie Rogers, *Emerging Woman*

Some of us take a long time to learn that leaning on others and asking for their help is courageous rather than shameful. When we do ask, we discover the support we seek has always been there. We realize others have trekked the byways that dismay us and can testify we too will survive and recover.

Yet they do not judge, nor do they project their paths onto us. They provide a safe audience for our stories, even when we tell the same stories every week. We discover the relief of dropping our masks and revealing our honest selves. We heal and move out of loneliness and isolation into grace, guilt-free and shame-free. We become part of a community of compassion.

> *I thank the Goddess for my experience of her through the support of others.*

APRIL 8

Vision

> *"The battle is to hold to the vision I know I*
> *must express, but the confidence to do it,*
> *where does that come from?"*
>
> Honor Moore,
> "My Grandmother Who Painted"

We cannot change what we do not see. We cannot have purpose without guiding visions. Having visions enables us to take charge of our lives instead of letting life happen to us. We can create visions of anything in our lives we want to change—residences, relationships, jobs, blocked creativity. How? We collect pictures of scenes that appeal to us, even when we're not sure why they do. We read, noting what works for us. We listen to the stories of others. We pay attention to dreams. We take uninterrupted time alone to ask what our souls crave. We project ourselves into the future—what would make us happiest five years from now? Ten? Twenty-five? What will we be doing? Where and how will we live? In heeding and fulfilling our visions, we model wholeness for our younger sisters.

I will create and trust my visions.

APRIL 9

Despair

*"Maggie had a sudden view of her life as
circular. It forever repeated itself, and it was
entirely lacking in hope."*

Anne Tyler, *Breathing Lessons*

*D*espair is feeling everything we do is in vain, useless, or ephemeral; feeling we have nothing to anticipate with hope or reflect on with pride or pleasure; feeling we have compromised or surrendered everything we ever wished for—to no useful purpose. Life becomes drudgery; like blind Samson, we forever grind away in the mill. When we feel ensnared in endless circles, we need to step outside them and view ourselves and our lives objectively.

Realizing the sterility of repetition helps lift despair. Hope lies in deviation and surprise. Being inconsistent, varying even such small things as exercise, diet, and recreation relieves despair. Even when we must repeat events and feelings, we remember we're not the same people as the first time, so they are never exactly the same.

*I will not go around in circles; I will lift myself
into a spiral.*

Fears from the Past

"Fear of what? I cannot say—& even at the time, I was never able to formulate my terror. It was like some dark undefinable menace. . . ."

Edith Wharton, "Life and I"

Fear can be a sensible reaction to a stimulus, but sometimes we unnecessarily fear things today because feelings engendered by past trauma still engulf us. A dog bit us when we were five; we refuse a weekend invitation from dog owners. A romance with a blond stock analyst ended traumatically; now we hesitate committing ourselves to a man nothing like the first—except that he's blond and analyzes stocks.

We can work on these fears by asking ourselves how old we feel when we experience them. If it's younger than our present age, we can take ourselves back to that age and deal with the frightening memories while reminding ourselves that we're grown up now.

I refuse to let past fears rule my life.

Living in the Present

> *"And every bird in the universe chittering,*
> *jabbering, clucking. . . . Just because it's*
> *today, today. With no thought of the future or*
> *past. Today. Hurray. Hurray!"*
>
> Sandra Cisneros, *"Bien* Pretty"

*H*ow much we miss by failing to live in the present. Rushing to decorate for Christmas on Thanksgiving weekend, we miss the relaxed gratitude of that holiday. Putting away Christmas on New Year's Day, we miss honoring the new year with quiet reflection. Anxious about completing a project, we miss the pleasure of its process.

Sometimes we have to be in nature or around animals, children, or elderly people to remember what a gift the present is, and how we must release worries, lists, and goals to receive it.

Living in the present increases happiness and decreases worries. Tomorrow I have a meeting I dread, but right now, I have a cup of steaming fragrant tea on my desk, and I'm comfortable in my clothes. That's enough.

I'm grateful for this present moment.

Reality

"She tested our strength to establish realities."
Maxine Hong Kingston, *The Woman Warrior*

We midlife women are based in reality. Our fantasies and dreams give us pleasure, but we never abandon reality to sink into the fantastic for long. We've given up some of the impossible goals of our youth—that we'd always weigh 110 pounds, someday we'd wake up with naturally curly hair, in time the vicious relative would soften.

Being realistic does not mean relinquishing our visions or ignoring a rainbow because of the misery of the flooded street. It means realizing what is apt to be accomplished, thus making it easier for us to go ahead and do it. We don't try to evade reality with drugs or alcohol or self-delusion. We just do the best we can with what we have—in the real world.

Reality is what I have to work with; I make the most of it.

Home

*"Where we come from in America no longer
signifies—it's where we go, and what we do
when we get there, that tells us who we are."*

Joyce Carol Oates,
The New Yorker, 8 May 1995

Our family has had seventeen different homes, never living in one house longer than seven years. When people ask "Where's home?" we respond, "Wherever we live."

Certainly nomadic living has disadvantages. Our sons couldn't show their brides the trees they fell from or a wall recording their growth in pencil marks. My husband and I can't decide where we want our mortal remains buried (him) or strewn (me). I've said too many good-byes to kind neighbors, left too many flowers uncut, and expended too much energy repainting, redecorating, remodeling, and replanting.

Yet we who move frequently learn to make homes and friends anywhere. Family rituals and ties are strengthened. And we identify ourselves by who we are and what we do, rather than where we're from.

I can flourish wherever I am planted.

Grief

"Only . . . women whose eyes have been washed clear with tears . . get the broad vision."

Dorothy Dix, *Dorothy Dix, Her Book*

When we have suffered agonizing loss, and grief rakes us with sharp claws, we cry often and long. We demand to know why our hearts had to be broken. We may experience wild mood and behavior changes, one moment destroying reminders of our loss, and the next hugging the fragments to our hearts. The first stage of grief involves experiencing and expressing it fully because grief trapped in the heart can metamorphose into anger.

Then we can choose to endure, even though endurance means suffering. Finally, we can choose to begin living again. But no one can tell us how long we should—or will—stay in each stage.

When we allow ourselves to work through grief, we will be comforted. Eventually, we will feel like resuming our usual work; we may even feel a release of creative energy.

I will be gentle with myself in grief.

Meditation

"We meditate to discover our own identity, our right place in the scheme of the universe."

Julia Cameron, *The Artist's Way*

In meditation we empty ourselves and are made full. Meditation restores and rejuvenates us by connecting us with the wellsprings of love and compassion in the universe. Meditation grants us full access to our energy and power and helps us solve problems that our conscious mind cannot. We often come out of meditation knowing what to do. We don't know how we reached the answer, but we know intuitively it is right and it will work.

Meditation permits us to honor the universe and ourselves. It takes us on spiritual vacations from which we return refreshed and renewed. It teaches us to let go and also makes us more mindful. In meditation, we breathe in the golden light of health and wholeness and breathe out the darkness of pain and suffering and hatred.

Meditating nourishes my spirit. I will try to make meditation part of my routine.

Retirement

"The successful woman retiree has usually planned for her postretirement years."
Jane Porcino, *Growing Older, Getting Better*

*W*omen face retirement with more equanimity than men, probably because we've engaged in patterns of engagement/disengagement for most of our lives, shifting careers to accommodate the geographical moves of our partners, taking time out from careers to rear children or care for parents, returning to school.

Planning financially for retirement starts now as we figure how much disposable income we will need then, calculate how much we should set aside now, and what changes, if any, we should make in our current lifestyles. If we want to continue working after sixty-five, we need to be aware that "retiring into work" can be financially penalized and prepare for that. If a second career will require more education, we start taking classes now. If retirement will require changing locations, we start researching other geographical areas now.

Planning for retirement now will ease the process then.

Happiness

> *"One is happy as a result of one's own efforts,*
> *once one knows the necessary ingredients of*
> *happiness—simple tastes, a certain degree of*
> *courage, self-denial to a point, love of work,*
> *and above all, a clear conscience."*
>
> George Sand [Amandine Lucile Aurore
> Dupin], *Correspondence*, Vol. 5

What makes some of us happy does not evoke happiness in others. George Sand's definition makes no mention of loving or being loved, an essential ingredient in happiness for many of us.

To be happy, we must decide to be happy. We might begin by giving up judging ourselves and others. We can live authentically. We can be present, asking ourselves often, "What would make me happy *right now*?" and, when possible, doing exactly that. Happiness may involve sacrifice or trade-offs. Anna Quindlen left her job as a columnist for the *New York Times* to be home with her children and write novels. She says she gave up status and fame but gained happiness.

I was born to be happy.

Crying

> "A tear, heard by anyone of heart, is
> understood as a cry to come closer."
>
> Clarissa Pinkola Estés,
> Women Who Run with the Wolves

My friend Jan cries easily—at weddings, at reunions, at holiday celebrations. Her facile tears made me uneasy until I learned to cry myself and realized how crying softens the heart, making it possible to respond to others. It's no coincidence that everyone wants to be Jan's friend.

Too many of us are ashamed of our tears, regarding them as signs of weakness rather than trusting them as true indicators of our deepest feelings. Some situations, injustices, and slights call for crying as wholeheartedly as we did as children. In expressing our pain—and our joy—through tears, we find relief. How differently might we live and relate to others if we accepted our tears as our teachers? What changes might we make in our world?

*When I need to cry, I will not allow my tears to
shame me.*

Taking Risks

> *"If we do not risk, if we play prescribed social
> roles instead of taking our journeys we feel . . .
> an emptiness inside."*
>
> Carol Pearson, *The Hero Within*

Many of us take more risks now, breaking free from our familial or societal roles and journeying spiritually or physically to mystical places of adventure and wonder. We've discovered that if we don't dare a little danger now and then, if we always stay on safe, familiar paths, we can't express our creativity and our wisdom.

We're willing to follow our dreams—go on a vision quest, spend three days in a silent retreat, send a children's story to an agent. We're willing to try the unfamiliar—eat exotic cuisine, wear a hat to the opera, learn to ski. We're willing to share our vulnerability with others, risk being laughed at, do things others might consider foolish. We're willing to risk what we are for what we might be.

To dare is to live.

Hate

*"I know well that hate is a consuming fire
poisoning every part of us, yet . . . some
degree of it is as cleansing as fire."*

Florida Scott-Maxwell,
The Measure of My Days

*H*atred directed toward injustice, corruption, and evil can purify, purging us of minor irritations and concerns, focusing our energy, giving our lives purpose. Impersonal hatred can even be creative. Yet we have to take care to control our passionate hatred.

When we hate something because it's different or because we fear it, then we might try understanding it instead. When we hate others, we might ask ourselves to what degree our hatred is self-hate. Have we projected our own undesirable traits onto them? As Pogo so famously said, "We have met the enemy and he is us." Are our enemies our reflections? If so, we can use our animosity to get to know ourselves better.

*I can use my hate to reform society — and
myself.*

Scarcity/Abundance

"Since everyone can draw on the universal supply, we deprive no one with our abundance."

Julia Cameron, *The Artist's Way*

*E*ven though we have tasted abundance, sometimes we find ourselves fearing scarcity—financial, material, and emotional. Although the universe has proven time after time that its gifts are infinite and generative, we act as though all good things are finite and limited. When we think the good fortune of others means less for us, we can't rejoice in their blessings.

Our fear of potential neediness begins in infancy when we wait too long for a soft breast or a warm bottle. How hungrily we snatch it when it arrives, how greedily we suck. Yet our adult experiences confirm a universe generally willing to provide what we *need* (if not always what we *want*). So when ancient greediness stirs, we remember that there is more than enough to go around, and we will receive a fair portion.

I will not fear famine during a time of abundance.

Housework

"Housekeeping, the art of the infinite, is no game for amateurs."

Ursula K. Le Guin, "Sur"

What bothers us the most about housework is its infiniteness. No matter how tightly made the beds, how sparkling clean the counters, how dust-free the shelves, sooner rather than later, it's all to do over again. Yet there's something to be said for the mindless, repetitive tasks of housework. Finishing each is satisfying even when the results are ephemeral. Unlike many other jobs, housework chores have definite beginnings and endings. They seldom require supervision, and we can usually set our own schedules and priorities. Chores such as ironing can produce an altered state and loosen creative blocks. More vigorous jobs such as shampooing carpets or washing windows allow us to discharge energy and anger. And we can always hire out or negotiate what we can't—or won't—do.

I'm not a housewife because I didn't marry my house. I do live in it, however, so I don't mind doing some of its work.

Perfectionism

"If man was allowed to be infallible, I see no reason why the same privilege should not be extended to woman."

Maria Edgeworth, "An Essay on the Noble Science of Self-Justification"

No, we don't want to extend the quest for infallibility to woman because the compulsive perfectionist, the woman who cannot admit her humanity, her fallibility, is merciless, constantly berating herself for failures real and imagined. She broods over error, magnifying the simplest mistake into a dreadful sin. She cannot enjoy her accomplishments because if she is less than perfect in anything else, she fears losing her lifetime efforts. She is blind to her good qualities and sees only her errors. She assumes the rest of the world judges her as harshly as she judges herself. To protect herself against the anxiety of failure, sometimes she gives up and withdraws from life.

I will remember that if something is worth doing, it's probably worth doing badly.

Being Silenced

> "Let us never accept silence as our fate
> again!"
>
> Erica Jong,
> "My Grandmother on My Shoulder"

*A*s women many of us were gagged too long—told it wasn't polite to speak unless spoken to, told what we had to say was uninteresting, told to be quiet and smile. No longer will we permit ourselves to be silenced by tradition, convention, or opposition. We will be silent no longer. We realize that death will silence us in due time; for now we will shout out what and who we are. And we will speak for those who do not have the education to speak for themselves, for those whom poverty has muted, for those whose voices have been quieted by imprisonment and torture, for those too young or too old to be heard.

Silent no longer, I speak for myself and my sisters who cannot.

Sacrifice

"My dear child, you ought to know your value better, and not allow your life to be worried away for no earthly good—it is a sort of quixotism you have for sacrificing yourself. . . ."

Geraldine Jewsbury, *A Selection from the Letters to Jane Welsh Carlyle*

*E*liminating bad habits and addictions and purging ourselves of negativism are worthwhile sacrifices. But sacrificing to cover up others' mistakes or support their bad habits is harmful. Even sacrificing from love is wrong if we deplete ourselves completely. In Shel Silverstein's parable *The Giving Tree*, an apple tree sacrifices blossoms, shade, fruit, and branches for a boy. Fortunately, when all she has left is a stump, the boy has grown old and wants only to sit down. We may not be so lucky.

We should also consider our motivation for sacrifice. If we harbor expectations for an eventual payback, we may become bitter if it turns out we have martyred ourselves for nothing.

Before choosing to sacrifice, I will consider the cost very carefully.

Writing

"*When the courage to write finally comes, it may be simply because I have lived long enough.*"

Hortense Calisher, *Herself*

*W*e've discovered the value of writing something every day, that recording dreams, conversations, descriptions, and emotions does us good. Writing helps us heal old and current wounds, realize what we think and how we feel, remember who we were and anticipate who we are becoming.

Writing is such a simple pleasure because we can write anywhere, anytime. We write to enliven trips, explore dilemmas, create beauty, record impressions, surprise ourselves, and exorcise demons. We write what we never dare say, thoughts we even fear realizing we have.

We help our habit of keeping journals or diaries by reading books such as Julia Cameron's *The Artist's Way* and *The Artist's Way Workbook*, Tristine Ranier's *The New Diary*, Natalie Goldberg's *Writing Down the Bones* and *Wild Mind*, and Anne Lamott's *Bird by Bird*.

A writer within me waits for expression.

Coincidence/Synchronicity

> "Synchronicity, *a word coined by C. G. Jung*
> *to describe coincidences between our inner*
> *subjective world and outer events."*
>
> Jean Shinoda Bolen, *Crossing to Avalon*

One morning we think of a dear friend who lives abroad; that afternoon we receive a letter from her for the first time in many months. We've been considering pursuing a particular interest—in the same week, we receive a catalog listing courses in the field, we see a stack of books on it at the store, and, randomly surfing TV channels, we come across a program on it. Jungians call this synchronicity; others call such happy coincidences "God working anonymously."

We pay attention to coincidences. When we think of the same person three different times in a day in wholly unrelated situations, we call or write. If we continuously dream of mountains, we consider revising our plans for a beach vacation.

> *Sometimes coincidences are not coincidental; they*
> *represent a call to action.*

Apologizing

> *"Easier to travel a thousand miles and camp*
> *among strange tribes than it is to apologize."*
> Jean Thompson, "Driving to Oregon"

*S*aying a sincere "I'm sorry" sometimes chokes us. Admitting we have been wrong, implying we are imperfect terrifies us. Yet no one is perfect—in intent or action. When assuming responsibility for our lives, we relinquish defensiveness and accept that our conduct occasionally hurts others. We know we apologize primarily for ourselves. We cannot grow and develop without claiming all our efforts, both noble and ignoble. We can listen to those we have injured tell us how we have hurt them and redeem our mistakes by changing our behavior and correcting the problems we cause.

Some of us may apologize too much—for gifts, for generosity, even for taking up space. Needless apologizing is as toxic as the inability to apologize for real harm.

> *Apologizing honors and respects the rights of*
> *others while admitting misdeeds.*

Failure

"If we are not willing to fail we will never accomplish anything."

Madeleine L'Engle, *Two-Part Invention*

When the possibility of failure so intimidates us that we dwell by the fire instead of risking storm winds and dark forests, we lose our chance of finding treasure. Certainly failure hurts, injuring ego, pride, and security. But it isn't permanent unless we choose to make it so by staying down. How many times does a toddler learning to walk fall? Yet, grabbing the furniture or the nearest pair of legs, she hauls herself up, and launches herself into treacherous open space over and over. Sometimes she cries and, exhausted, quits for a bit. But soon there she goes again, letting go, spreading her arms for balance, taking off, achieving stability.

Failure teaches what not to do next time, who to trust, and what we need before we try again.

If I try, I may fail; if I don't try, I'll never know success.

God

> "Creativity cannot exist without the feminine
> principle, and I am sure God is not merely
> male or female but He-She—our Father-
> Mother God."
>
> Margaret Walker,
> "On Being Female, Black, and Free"

*M*argaret Walker's belief in the dual nature of God echoes the words of Julian of Norwich in the fourteenth century: "As truly as God is our Father, so is God our Mother . . . To the property of motherhood belong nature, love, wisdom and knowledge, and this is God." Mothers nourish their children and sacrifice themselves for them. Mothers model God as woman.

Many aspects of God remind us of the "feminine principle"—love and mercy, humility and meekness, service to others. Most of us are very certain that assuming divinity is masculine and thus excluding one-half of humanity from a share in that divinity, severely limits deity. God is our Father and God is our Mother.

> *God is all-knowing, all-loving, all-powerful.*
> *God is both Mother and Father.*

Hope

> *"I had again that quieting sense of the
> continuity of human experience on this earth,
> its perpetual aspirations, setbacks, failures
> and re-beginnings in eternal hope. . . ."*
>
> Katherine Anne Porter,
> "The Future Is Now"

We're never too grown up to stop hoping; to the contrary, a hopeful nature may be one of the qualities that keeps us young. When we hope, we believe even the most menial jobs have meaning. We can undertake the most onerous of responsibilities because we hope we won't have to do it forever.

Hope takes our hand when we feel we are alone. Hope helps us stand when sadness threatens to buckle us. Hope restores our energy when circumstances seem to defeat us. Hope glorifies the mundane. Hope gives us the courage to dare to be ourselves and to reveal ourselves to others.

To live in hope is to believe in light when it is dark, in beauty where ugliness abounds, in peace when conflict seems to reign.

Hope is an essential ingredient of my life.

Self-Deception

*"Most of our platitudes notwithstanding,
self-deception remains the most difficult
deception."*

Joan Didion, "On Self-Respect"

hen we were younger, we may have been able to fool ourselves. But as we mature, we find our capacity for self-deception and our willingness to practice it melting away. We face the mirror of ourselves, discarding the masks that announced "I am Mother, I am Wife, I am Professional Woman, I am Chairperson, I am Confidante; therefore, I exist."

Now we know better. We no longer depend on masks for our sense of self. We recognize when our roles are too restrictive and confining, when we have become deadened to anticipation and joy. We need pretend no longer. We have gazed unflinchingly into our depths and found darkness there as well as treasures beyond counting. We accept it all.

*I no longer practice self-deception; I know
myself to be flawed and precious.*

Compliance

"A life of compliance is a life of denial."
Starhawk, *Truth or Dare*

Once I dreamed that I was a tiny little woman with a bouffant hairdo,
struggling to keep a door locked against an enraged woman.
My therapist was matter-of-fact about the puzzling image,
saying it represented the person I once was, compliant,
sweet, subservient, anxious to please and accommodate, a
good corporate wife trying to keep the door shut against a
murderously angry self who would no longer be denied.

I didn't like the interpretation—but it fit. Perhaps too
many of us have spent far too long being compliant because
we thought it was the only way to survive in a patriarchal
society. Now we know that constantly subordinating our
needs and wishes to those of others soured and embittered
us. Our colleagues and families, accustomed to our sacrifices, took our compliance for granted. So we will be compliant no longer.

*From now on, I comply only with my own
demands.*

Forgiving

*"Perhaps the greatest measure of her soul is
how much she is able to forgive."*
Marion Woodman, *Leaving My Father's House*

orgiving to forget something we can't
bear to know numbs us. Yet forgiving
without forgetting, forgiving despite slights and injuries and
dreadful harm, forgiving in full knowledge of the damage
caused heals us.

Sometimes we forgive when no one has even asked for
our forgiveness because we forgive for ourselves, for the
good of our souls. It hurts us to carry grudges; bearing
resentment restricts us, too.

To forgive we first have to accept ourselves just as we
are—imperfect, flawed, mortal—and love ourselves. When
we love ourselves as damaged humans, then we can extend
that forgiving love to others. They have harmed us just as
we have harmed others. Yet, we—and they—are worthy of
forgiveness.

*When I forgive, I remember that I, too, deserve
forgiveness.*

Travel

"Travel always jogs the imagination."

Mairi MacInnes,
The New Yorker, 26 February/4 March 1996

The pleasures of travel are threefold; the travel itself, the planning and anticipation beforehand, and the afterglow of memory. Travel opens our eyes and our psyches; by experiencing the unfamiliar, we gain new insights. Changes in our perception affect us forever, so there is no substitute for the enrichment of traveling.

We consider traveling alone now. We've discovered that making our own arrangements, not knowing anyone on the sightseeing bus, wandering through a sun-filled park in a foreign city, responsible to no one, with no particular place to be at any particular time, is liberating. As we meet and conquer the predicaments and dilemmas of travel—lost bags, overcharges, unwanted attention, language barriers, and misunderstandings—we realize how much we can handle.

Travel enriches, strengthens, and revitalizes me.

Dependence

*"Only the psychologically less healthy women
remained as dependent and passive at fifty as
they had been in adolescence."*

Betty Friedan, *The Fountain of Age*

*L*iving in community, trusting and relying on others is positive dependence. But women who cannot bear solitude, who cannot manage the ordinary tasks of adult life, who cannot make decisions, exhibit the negative face of dependence. This dependence, necessary in childhood, charming in adolescence, becomes dispensable as we mature. The strongest of partners eventually tires of carrying the load of two; the weight of a parasitic vine topples the straightest, tallest pines.

If we depend a bit too much on others, leaving decisions and responsibilities to them that should be ours, it's time to become independent and learn to enjoy solitude, make choices, and carry our own packs—balancing the checkbook, calculating income tax, writing wills, and changing tires if necessary.

*I know when to rely on others and when to rely
on myself.*

Privacy

*"You should teach your . . . [daughters] to
think privacy . . . the happiest state of life."*
Lady Mary Wortley Montagu, *Letters*

*W*hy do people seem to regard a woman's closed door as a challenge while a man's closed door means "Do Not Disturb"? I feel the need for privacy strongly because I write at home. I've had to work hard to convince others that knocking at my closed door to ask if they can disturb me already has. I agree with Clarissa Pinkola Estés that speaking to a woman while she balances "a big cardhouse of ideas on a single fingertip . . . carefully connecting all the cards using tiny crystalline bones and a little spit . . . is to break her heart."

We must be allowed to take long aimless walks or drives—alone. We must have places to go to and rooms where no one will disturb us. We must convince those who love us and those who work with us that our doors cannot always be open.

*I will protect the privacy I need to nourish,
refresh, and renew myself.*

Rage

"*She is Murder Inc. inside her head, where her images of revenge are always merciless and swift and very permanent.*"

Judith Viorst, *Necessary Losses*

*N*ow we can acknowledge the icy-hot rage that sometimes burns within us, the urge to hurl Grandmother's translucent china piece after piece against a brick wall or sledgehammer someone's car. We used to swallow our rage, appearing as placid as sleeping puppies; only we knew our pit-bull potential.

Now we face our inner rage, learning where it comes from, what it feeds on, and what kind of treatment brings it to wrathful life. Expressing rage through destructive acts may be wrong, but rage itself is not. We seek its causes and work to eliminate those causes for our emotional and physical health. We discover safe ways to vent rage—pounding pillows, hitting tennis racquets against a bed, and writing letters that we never send.

When I control the fire of rage, it does not consume me; instead, it illuminates and warms me.

Expressing Negative Emotions

> *"Women are supposed to be very calm,*
> *generally: but women feel just as men*
> *feel. . . ."*

Charlotte Brontë, Jane Eyre

Our culture generally does not approve of women who express negative emotions by swearing. Yet those who exhibit temper usually are taken more seriously than those who don't. So in restraining ourselves from expressing emotions such as anger, we deny ourselves the possibility of being respected as individuals. If the worst that comes out of our mouth when a careless driver backs into our car or a heavy man steps on our foot is "oh dear," no one may believe we've been injured. Perhaps we don't choose to make vigorous cursing a regular habit, but a sharp emphatic "damn" or "shit" or even "f . . k" can be liberating—and can gain us some respect. So we need to give ourselves permission to voice frustration, hostility, and anger—when they're called for.

> *Giving voice to negative emotions liberates*
> *them—and me.*

Being Mothered

"An image of woman mothering her children,
mothering herself, rooted in her own strength,
substance, and wisdom. . . ."

Judith Duerk, *Circle of Stones*

On the fourth Sunday in Lent, the English observe "Mothering Sunday." People can buy cards honoring anyone who has ever mothered them—friends, teachers, colleagues, employers. Many of us are fortunate enough to have been mothered by other women as well as by our biological mothers. Women connected to us because they shared our thoughts, visions, and values. We could also choose a day to honor these "mothering" women—the high school English teacher who praised our first attempts at verse, the older sister who taught us about menstruation, the friend who took our children when we had pneumonia, the boss who mentored us through a complex assignment. We can also remember to mother ourselves so that we nurture, encourage, and influence others from our strength and security.

I can mother and be mothered, and I can
mother myself.

Flexibility

*"Even if I made an inane and stupid choice, I
stuck by it rather than 'be like a woman and
change my mind.'"*

Maya Angelou,
Wouldn't Take Nothing for My Journey Now

Wʜen we fear being considered women who can't make up our minds, sometimes we adhere stubbornly to decisions and positions that no longer serve just because we always have . . . cooked a roast on Sundays, voted a straight ticket, mailed Christmas cards four weeks early. Yet, flexibility doesn't mean following every new trend in fashion, food, or politics. It doesn't mean giving up core values. It means giving up control, letting go, and letting others occasionally take charge.

We recognize the value of flexibility because we know that those who cannot adapt may be left behind. As flexible women of fifty, we view the world objectively, acknowledging, welcoming, and embodying change.

*I can bend in the breeze without uprooting my
sense of self.*

Regret

"Just regret, gripping me like a steel claw."
Bebe Moore Campbell, *Sweet Summer*

*R*egret fills us with remorse for what we did, said, and lost that we shouldn't have, as well as remorse for what we didn't do, say, or lose that we should have. When we're trudging along in the inexorable cycle of "if only," we need to realize that what might have been different wasn't, and won't be. Some things turn out well, some things don't. Some doors close, other doors open. Sometimes we're responsible for what happens, and sometimes we're not.

Regret spurs us to change. We resolve that outcomes we can affect will be different next time. And then we let go and get on with life. Otherwise regret becomes a barrier convincing us not to try anything for fear we might live to regret it. But, after all, maybe we won't.

Regret wastes energy. If I must, I'll give myself five minutes for regrets—and then move on.

Humor

"*The Human Tribe needs to be shown how to use humor to diffuse potentially painful or destructive situations.*"

Jamie Sams, *The 13 Original Clan Mothers*

*H*umor blesses us because laughing at ourselves, admitting that life has ridiculous and serious moments, parody and poetry, banana peels and Bach, guarantees longer and more pleasant lives. Those in the most serious of professions—ministry, therapy, medicine—often have a great sense of humor. We're aware that events and people who irritate and anger us will often seem funny in retrospect, so we can try to achieve enough distance to lighten tense situations by laughing now.

Sometimes we take ourselves so seriously, insisting so fervently on respect, that we exclude the joy of shared laughter over common foibles. When we join in laughter, we know we are with soul mates; laughter bonds us with others as surely as common causes and interests.

It's sensible to have a sense of humor.

Letting Go

*"Attachment is the great fabricator of illusions;
reality can be attained only by someone who
is detached."*

Simone Weil, *Gravity and Grace*

uddhists teach nonattachment;
Christians, "God's will be done";
twelve-step recovery groups, "let go, let God." Letting go
acknowledges we can't control or solve everything. We know
we cannot make others change, so we quit manipulating
them to get what we want. We say good-bye to projects,
relationships, and aspects of our lives that are finished.

We've learned how to let go. When my friend Sally no
longer wants to struggle with an issue, she writes it down
and places the paper in her "God box," symbolically turning the decision over to God. And when we let go, we usually find everything moves along just fine. It takes less
energy, after all, to relax and release than it does to struggle to hold on.

*When I let go of something, I release myself for
other work.*

Suffering

*"In silence shall women suffer and struggle,
the minister said so often—and there is
something so beautiful in that thought, he
added."*

Dikken Zwilgmeyer, "An Everyday Story"

No, there's nothing beautiful about silent, passive suffering, especially suffering caused by victimization. It's an obscenity, one we try to prevent because we know suffering can devastate, crushing energy and joy. Suffering can embitter, turning its victims mean and vindictive.

But if suffering must be, there can be consolation. Suffering can be an opportunity to grow and learn. Sometimes it is only possible to reach the truth—about ourselves or others—by traveling the path of pain. And when we make that journey, when we begin to understand what causes our suffering, then we can alleviate it, and we can begin to heal.

I do not choose suffering, but if I must suffer, I will learn from it.

Intelligence

"Use your brains. . . . Once you make that
mistake, of being—distracted, over a man,
your life will never be your own."
Alice Munro, *Lives of Girls and Women*

The quandary that faced us as girls—
how to acknowledge and use our
brains and still attract guys—unfortunately still remains an
issue. Studies show girls today begin "dimming down" their
abilities in prepuberty. Why do they get "distracted" from
their intelligence by the opposite sex? Apparently some still
operate with the belief that males do not want to be thought
less intelligent than their partners.

We need to show these young women what we know:
Maintaining a pose of dimness is difficult, and few specta-
cles are more sad than bright young women feigning stu-
pidity. It's preferable to use the beacon of intelligence to
attract, establish, and maintain partnerships of responsible,
competent, and wise equals.

I use my intelligence to enrich my life and the
lives of those around me.

Play

"The one you wanted to be
is the one you are. Come play. . . ."
Jean Valentine, "The One You Wanted to Be
Is the One You Are"

*Y*es! Come out and play today. We're proud of our accomplishments, but we know if we work continuously, we will lose our zest. Play breaks renew our psyches and enrich our souls. Play is whatever gives us most pleasure: painting, bird watching, photography, quilting, amateur theater, mountain climbing, line dancing. We can play with our pets and turn ordinary activities into play. Walks become treasure hunts if we turn over logs, rocks, and driftwood to see what secrets they hide. If our imagination needs inspiration, we can ask children along.

Whatever we do in play, we may need to be reminded not to make play our work. We won't restrict play or time it or limit our fun with concern for our appearance.

Play is joyful abandonment of duty — and just
as necessary for my soul as productive work.

Balance

*"I must find a balance somewhere, or an
alternating rhythm between . . . extremes. . . ."*
Anne Morrow Lindbergh, *Gift from the Sea*

*W*e all contain within ourselves contra-rieties: love and hate, animal and divine, defiance and passivity, independence and dependence. Balance is our chief operating officer, the chairman who manages our opposites, permitting now one and then another dominance. Yet, balance does not mean living our lives in the safe middle; rather, it means the ability to move from side to side, now going north, then south, now traveling in the fast lane, then slowing down.

Balance aims at permitting all of our selves appropriate expression—playful child, sulky adolescent, loving and giving mother, crafty competitor, wise leader. Balance aspires to develop all of our energies—physical, mental, creative, spiritual, emotional—rather than overdeveloping one to the exclusion of the others.

*I can achieve balance by not denying any of my
selves.*

Honesty

"Ah, the great moral conflict in life—honesty or kindness?"

> Judith Martin, *Miss Manners' Guide to Excruciatingly Correct Behavior*

*L*iving authentic lives requires honesty and courage. We used to be dishonest to avoid hurting others, but we discovered that the persons we most feared hurting were actually ourselves. We were afraid to face the consequences of our honesty. When we said honestly, "No, I don't want to contribute to your cause or teach that class or chair that committee or task force," we feared what people might think of us. They didn't understand, and they did protest, and sometimes we were estranged and lonely for a while. But we also earned grudging respect for our courage and honesty. Eventually, we gained a reputation as truth-tellers. Those who wanted flattery and insincerity sought it elsewhere, while those who wanted honesty came to us.

I am honest, especially with myself.

Miracles

"How in varying degrees each of us starts to believe
In miracles when faced with the world's luster."
Maurya Simon, "Crèche"

*M*iracles are events that human reason and understanding do not lead us to expect—the return of a stolen purse with credit cards and cash intact, surviving an airplane crash, living through the eye of a hurricane. Receiving miracles differs from simply being lucky or fortunate because we believe a supernatural power affected the outcome. Yet why shouldn't we expect goodness and kindness from strangers or trust the sturdiness of the airplane and the training of its crew or believe in the stability of our houses?

Perhaps we should open ourselves to the possibility of miracles; perhaps we should even expect them. We allow the possibility of divine intervention when we give up our wills and wishes for our happiness in exchange for the greatest good for the greatest number.

Miracles happen every day; help me become aware of them.

Choices

*"The true cost of anything is what we give up
in order to have it. It is the path not taken."*
Jean Shinoda Bolen,
Goddesses in Everywoman

*E*very day presents us with choices from the simple—is it warm enough to wear the peach linen suit?—to the difficult—should I quit my job and free-lance? In the middle of complex choices, we remind ourselves that the ability to choose is a gift. When we can choose, we can control our actions.

Deciding between alternate courses of action involves listing pros and cons, seeking expert advice, *and* relying on intuition. Choices that involve risk require courage. Choices that mandate great change test our commitment to process. And, as Bolen reminds us, choice always involves sacrifice: a book not read, a friendship forfeited, a relationship ended, a career not pursued.

*The freedom to choose carries the responsibility
to choose wisely.*

Birthdays

"Each birthday brings . . potentiality. . . ."
Jean Shinoda Bolen, *Crossing to Avalon*

*L*et's wish ourselves birthdays full of creativity, peace, and bliss. And let's honor our birthdays with honesty. Because birthdays are the one day a year some of us claim our age, what if, on our birthdays, we all wore attractive lapel pins, embellished with our favorite colors, which boldly stated our age *and* our weight? What if we decided to wear those pins not just on our birthdays but every day? What would that be like for us and for our younger and older sisters? Would there be such a powerful, collective sigh of relief that all the hair coloring, diet aids, girdles, and alpha-hydroxy acid products would blow right off the shelves and out of our homes? Shall we try it?

Happy birthday to me. I'm glad to be here, just the way I am.

Rebirth

*"Although endings are inevitable, they are
necessary for rebirths."*

Helena Maria Víramontes, "The Moths"

s we age, new passions replace former passions. We sublimate some of
our desires and gain new vitality for other interests. Something dies, something else is reborn. Life is fluidity and
change, and nothing remains fixed. As we make the passage
from one age to another, some of the roles we have played
that have been very important to us begin to decline and
die. We give up our large suburban homes and become mis-
tresses of city apartments and retirement cottages. No
longer the "youngest" at almost anything, we die to that role
and are reborn to wisdom.

Rebirth can be as painful as birth usually is, but once we
traverse the passage, we find new worlds to explore with
interesting people in them. Each age has its own rewards.
Welcome to the rebirth of fifty!

*Every ending, every death, leads to a new
beginning, a rebirth.*

Certainty/Uncertainty

"It might be unconscious organic certainty of getting through."

Dorothy Richardson, "The Ordeal"

*H*ow we long for certainty about the outcome of events, the reliability of those we trust, the happiness of those we love. We work hard to create these certainties. And sometimes we feel personal failure when events do not turn out as we planned, when those we trust betray us, and when people we've tried so hard to make happy are unhappy instead.

Yet it is the very uncertainty of what we value most, even life, that gives it value. Realizing that truth helps us accept uncertainty. For underneath all temporary uncertainty lies certainty: We do the best we can, we respect ourselves as human beings, and we believe our existence has purpose and value.

Uncertainty is a human condition, but I am certain I am intended to live my life to the fullest.

Gossip

"The business of her life was to get her daughters married; its solace was visiting and news."

Jane Austen, *Pride and Prejudice*

When I was a girl, I loved sitting in my grandmother's warm steamy kitchen after a holiday dinner and listening to the women in the family gossip. I learned a great deal about my extended family—and life as a woman. Although the word *gossip* to some connotes malice and sensationalism, it originally meant "godparent" and later, "friend," especially a woman. Sharing news, feelings, knowledge, and experience through gossip is a pleasurable pastime. Gossip is personal and particular and perhaps occasionally even petty, but not harmful (unless it aims to be hurtful).

Men sometimes frustrate us with their inattention to gossipy detail and their insistence on facts alone. Gossip colors and shades the pictures that facts only outline in black and white.

Gossip strengthens and nurtures relationships; it's an important means of communication.

Ecology

*"I pledge allegiance to the earth
and all its forms and expressions of life. . . ."*
Veronica Ray, *Green Spirituality*

$\mathcal{C}$aring for Mother Earth is not just good for her but good for us. When we pollute streams, level forests, and deplete the ozone layer, we pollute, damage, and exhaust our souls. We were not given the earth to despoil but to cherish. We fulfill our obligation to our first mother by recycling, planting rather than cutting down, doing business with "green" companies, walking instead of driving short distances, and supporting politicians who revere the earth as we do.

We can remember future generations and balance our desires against their needs. As women we have a natural affinity for the earth; we must protect and support her for those who will come after us.

I will do one thing today for the good of the earth.

Integrity

"But she cannot help feeling that she has been betrayed irreparably by the disunion between her way of living and her feeling of what life should be. . . ."

Katherine Anne Porter, "Flowering Judas"

Seeking integrity can be extremely difficult. Those we love and those who love us cannot always follow our paths; our separation from them causes all of us pain. And those who do not care for us may make light of our efforts for integrity or belittle them, especially when those efforts prove inconvenient for them. We may have to be alone more than we would like.

However, the pains of living an inauthentic life are probably worse. Trying to be what we think we ought to be rather than what we are, trying to please others rather than ourselves leads to feelings of fragmentation, separation, dissociation, and even betrayal.

Integrity is not a luxury; it's a necessity.

Change

"I guess I changed and he didn't."
Blanche Passa, quoted in Naomi Dunavan,
Houston Chronicle, 23 July 1995

Blanche and Jake Passa, married forty-eight years, have lived side by side in separate houses for five years. She has pioneered a new style of marriage. Changes in our society demand new behaviors; former methods become obsolete and old habits no longer effective, so new forms evolve. At fifty, we may straddle the line between old and new, some days clinging close to the familiar, other days leaping to embrace the unfamiliar. But whether we want or seek, or even think we need, change, changes in society will occur.

We wonder if we are stuck in ineffective patterns, if something else might be possible, so we may want to view our lives and experiences with fresh eyes. Change can be growth; when we feel content after making a change, we know that particular change was good for us.

I'm just the right age to welcome change.

Female Heroes

"What quest is worth pursuing?"
Amy Lowell, "From One Who Stays"

*D*eep within us lie the spirit, courage, and risk-taking sense of adventure of female heroes such as the astronaut Shannon Lucid. We're ready to be catapulted into space, to ride into battle, to rescue someone. But if we face every situation as though the outcome depends on us alone, if we expect those we save "to do it our way" from now on and be grateful, then perhaps we'd better rethink our roles as female heroes.

We can make our quests more meaningful by making them individual and personal. We can face down our interior ghosts and dragons to win the treasure of integrated and authentic personalities. Then we can share that treasure with our community, *if* the community wishes it.

Living an authentic life is heroic.

Energy

"An emphasis on female energy is needed to
restore the balance in the lives and psyches of
both women and men."

Hallie Austen Iglehart, *WomenSpirit*

In our fifties we find ourselves filled
with renewed energy and zest for living. We've learned how to delegate responsibility, we've
eliminated what drains our energy, and we've set new priorities that include taking care of ourselves. So we feel rejuvenated. If we do not, then we may want to examine our
lives and see what we're doing that we'd rather not. When
we give up trying to control others, we have more energy.
When we live authentically, giving up denial, defense, and
deceptions, we have more energy.

We feel most alive when we are passionate about work,
social activities, friendships, politics, and relationships. Passion feeds our energy.

*The more energy I expend on what I believe in,
the more energy I have.*

Vacations

> *"Mothers and housewives are the only workers*
> *who do not have regular time off. They are*
> *the great vacationless class."*
>
> Anne Morrow Lindbergh, *Gift from the Sea*

$\mathcal{W}$e need vacations—variety, travel, breaks in routines, new experiences. Time to spend a whole day with a book, time for long walks and afternoon naps, time in front of a single painting, time for lingering over dinner, and time to listen to loved ones.

And yet we cannot schedule vacations every week. Or can we? If we wish we could be our relaxed and happy vacation selves more of the time, perhaps we need to consider minivacations rather than living all year for long vacations. If what we treasure most about vacations is new experiences, why can't we try something new once a week? If what we enjoy most on vacations is relaxation, why can't we spend a weekend a month making no plans and doing nothing? If what we most enjoy is pressure-free time with loved ones, why can't we regularly set aside time for uninterrupted conversation?

Vacations are so valuable, I'm going to take
more of them.

Listening

> *"This is a game . . . in which each of us only listens to a little bit of what the other is saying."*
>
> Michelene Wandor, "Meet My Mother"

*L*istening, trying to understand what we hear, is a skill that improves with age. We no longer are so full of ourselves that we want only to talk, never to listen. We no longer feel the need to bring every conversation back to ourselves as often and quickly as possible. We now realize how much we learn by listening. Listening with open hearts and becoming aware of how what we are hearing affects us, we absorb the relevance of what is being said. This is the principle behind the "no cross-talk" rules of many recovery groups.

Misunderstandings result when we listen only partially, hearing only what we want to hear rather than what has actually been said. We have trained ourselves to be better listeners by asking what conversational partners require from us—interpretation, judgment, decisions, advice, or an echo.

Listening is often better for me than talking.

Intimacy

"We commonly confuse closeness with sameness and view intimacy as the merging of two separate 'I's' into one world view."

Harriet Goldhor Lerner,
The Dance of Intimacy

Intimacy requires a strong awareness of who we are and what we want as well as the ability to look at the desires of our intimates. Intimacy involves compromising and negotiating a mutually satisfying path. Intimacy is choosing to spend time with those whose identity we vow to protect and cherish rather than submerging individuality into identities as couples or best friends. We probably do not share all of the goals and values of our closest friends, but we can permit them to be themselves. We can enjoy being together without trying to make them mirror images of us. One can golf while the other sunbathes, and we can share dinner and conversation.

Intimacy protects two distinct personalities within a loving and supportive relationship.

Centeredness

*"Centred in self yet not unpleased to
please . . ."*

Christina Rossetti, "In Progress"

     taying centered in our materialistic
world is sometimes difficult. We need
time each day to bring ourselves to our soul centers by
prayer, meditation, and quiet reflection. We might choose
to ritualize this time by going to the same physical place at
the same time every day, playing the same music, or lighting the same candle. Or perhaps we always begin our centering time by reciting the same prayer or favorite
affirmation.

When we feel anxiety or frustration causing us to lose
our centeredness, we can sit quietly wherever we are, relax
our shoulders, necks, and jaws, take a few deep breaths, and
remind ourselves that we are strong, talented, capable
women. For we know that when we are centered in self,
everything is possible; we radiate autonomy, peace, and
wholeness.

Centeredness is not selfish; it's pragmatic.

Intuition

*"Women's growing reliance on their intuitive
processes is . . . an important adaptive move
in the service of self-protection, self-assertion,
and self-definition."*

Mary Belenky *et al.*,
Women's Ways of Knowing

Sometimes we denigrate our female gift of intuition. We attempt to lead logical, rational lives, and discount the value of our sixth sense. When we listen to and trust this inner truth, we gain a new source of wisdom and strength to share with our communities.

Intuition saves us from trouble and disaster. When we instinctively recoil from a person, an idea, or a suggestion, we should explore our uneasiness. What or whom does this event or person remind us of? Once my husband invited me to dinner with a man he was thinking of hiring. The evening was pleasant enough, but something about the man's behavior made me uneasy and I mentioned that later. Some background checking revealed a résumé padded to the point of fraudulence.

*I'm fortunate to have intuition as well as logic
and common sense to guide me.*

Living with Paradox

> *"The crone never sets up an either/or situation.*
> *She's lived too long to believe in a black and*
> *white world; she loves the many shades of*
> *gray."*
>
> Marion Woodman, *Leaving My Father's House*

We used to see the world as either/or—black *or* white, good *or* bad, friends *or* enemies. Now we accept paradox as an inevitable part of life; now we live in a both/and world, a world neither good nor bad but both. It contains injustice, violence, and suffering, *and* acts of kindness, tenderness, and self-sacrifice. Events that seem at first to be failures (a son not accepted by his father's fraternity) may turn into successes (he becomes the president of another fraternity). Few things in and of themselves are purely good or totally bad; our good fortune may depend on someone's misfortune, our happiness on someone's misery. It might have been easier to make decisions when we saw the world as either/or, but that restricted, narrow view was unfair to the richness and diversity of the actual world.

Accepting paradox is part of living life fully.

Codependence

> "A codependent person is one who has let
> another person's behavior affect him or her,
> and who is obsessed with controlling that
> person's behavior."
>
> Melodie Beattie, *Codependent No More*

Sometimes we've confused codependency with our instinct to nurture others and protect the weak. Staying home with a partner who has a high fever and uncontrollable vomiting is nurturing; calling him sick when he has a hangover is codependency. Taking pride in our partner's achievements is natural; talking exclusively about them instead of our own is codependency.

Codependency denotes weak or missing self-esteem. When we could not depend on ourselves for fulfillment of our needs, we may have focused on the needs of others and told ourselves we felt good doing that. And we may have used those overly solicitous actions to control them; because we had done so much more than was expected, they owed us. In midlife maturity, we can quit living through others.

I'm responsible for my own actions; so are those with whom I live and work.

Denial

> *"They are asking you to deny your*
> *experiences, which is to pretend that you do*
> *not exist and never have existed."*
>
> Rebecca West, "Parthenope"

*D*enial is like an avalanche; once it starts, it's hard to control. We deny our hunger, we deny our sorrow over unjust criticism or a friend's betrayal, we deny our unhealthy relationships. And soon we no longer trust our instincts: We don't know whether we're hungry or not, we don't recognize when we're hurt, and we don't know how to gauge a healthy relationship.

Denial is a hurtful habit that usually fools no one. Those who pretend with us often are fully aware of what we conceal. In that case, it's no longer a kindness to them or to us to continue the charade of denial.

Denial is being dishonest with myself. I want to see and live the truth of my life today and every day.

Parenting Our Parents

"So here am I at fifty, whiplashed between the generations."

Erica Jong, *Fear of Fifty*

*A*t fifty we can be mother and grandmother, daughter and granddaughter—and feel trapped between competing generational needs. Because 75 percent of caregivers are female relatives, we may find ourselves caring for aging parents. Maintaining balance between managing their lives and living our own is difficult. We don't want to neglect our nuclear family or let guilt deplete our lives. We may feel whatever we do is not enough—and too much.

Caring for parents has benefits—returning what they provided for us, sharing their final days, and living the maxim that families take care of families. But we must not be afraid to ask for help, to speak up when situations become intolerable, and to refuse to make financial, emotional, and physical sacrifices that are beyond us.

Help me to be as gentle with my aging parents as I would be with a child—and just as determined to preserve some time and energy for myself.

Jealousy

> *"The secret envy inside me is maybe the worst thing about my life. I am the Saddam Hussein of jealousy."*
>
> Anne Lamott, *Operating Instructions*

*J*ealousy is insidious and destructive— and omnipresent. No matter how much we own, some people will always have more. No matter how hard we try to keep ourselves attractive, there will always be more beautiful women with better bodies. No matter how hard we work, others who don't appear to work as hard will be more successful.

We can recognize jealousy and give ourselves time and privacy to cry or scream about how unfair life is. Then we remember that nobody promised it would be fair. Taking a good look around, we see those who also have less than we do, again for no apparent reason. It's just the way the world works. All we can do is be grateful for what we have, use it wisely, and accept that some will always have more—and some less.

It's OK to express jealousy, but I won't let it poison my life.

Detachment

*"She was so exceedingly tranquil . . . she gave
an impression of impermanence. . . . Nonattachment . . . was the word. The spiritual
become non-attached."*

Sylvia Townsend Warner,
"But at the Stroke of Midnight"

certain attitude of detachment can
be exceedingly helpful when we are
constantly harassed by advertising, recorded music,
machines that beep for attention, telephone solicitors, and
unsought social contacts. When we are stressed, it's nice to
detach—shut the door, ignore the telephone, reject the
unwanted friendship, and end an unproductive conversation. It's nice to concentrate on our spiritual rather than
our material selves.

For when we invest our hearts and souls and energies
into every cause, relationship, and project, we become
exhausted and depleted. We must be able to choose the most
important and then detach ourselves from the rest, letting
go of the nonessential.

*I am both a material and a spiritual being,
attached to some objects of this world and
detached from others.*

Leisure

"I sit for many hours . . . doing nothing, only
looking out at the flowers and the birds. My
thoughts come and go."
Ruth Prawer Jhabvala, "The Man with a Dog"

We need leisure to develop fully our capacities and talents. We need time to daydream, to stare idly out the window, watching the clouds form pictures. Yet as workdays and commuting time increase, time for leisure seems to evaporate. Or leisure activities become as compulsive as work: thirty minutes for aerobics, forty-five minutes to walk, thirty minutes to read professional journals.

Our souls require periods of unstructured idleness, chunks of time "doing" nothing, just "being." If we allow ourselves leisure, we will find clarity for decisions, solutions to problems, and access to knowledge we didn't realize we had. We can be truly ourselves, no longer bound by work or relationships or anyone else's sense of who we are.

*I will set aside some time each day for
cultivating my soul with leisure.*

Compassion

"With compassion, we see benevolently our own human condition and the condition of our fellow beings. We drop prejudice. We withhold judgment."

Christina Baldwin, *Life's Companion, Journal Writing as a Spiritual Quest*

To achieve compassion we must begin by forgiving ourselves for what might have been, or should have been, but wasn't. Then compassion can expand our hearts and souls, opening them up to others. We can begin to feel for them, to see as they see, to hurt as they hurt, and to heal them when it is within our power to do so. Compassion is more than pity and doesn't stop with feeling sorry for others. Compassion implies action. Tears for others are nice, but spending time with them, listening without judgment, making telephone calls on their behalf, and providing money also may be necessary.

Compassion is expansion; I embrace others as I embrace myself.

Humility

"I have often wished I had time to cultivate modesty. . . . But I am too busy thinking about myself."

Dame Edith Sitwell, *Observer*, 30 April 1950

What breathtaking confidence! Too often we have adopted a pose of humility and modesty that in our hearts we did not believe. Because we considered maidenly modesty one of the greatest virtues of a woman, we have waited for others to recognize and promote our good qualities. And we have felt resentful and bitter when they did not.

We have every right to be proud of our accomplishments and speak up when we feel they are being ignored or overlooked. Let us claim what is ours. The tiny flower blooming unseen in a rocky crevice pleases no one; the gorgeous scarlet rose carefully displayed in a window facing a busy street brings pleasure to many.

Modesty is becoming only when it is not false.

Compromise

"I realized that life entailed a series of
compromises of the private self to the public,
a slow accommodation to ordinariness, to
convention's momentum."

Joan Connor, "Broken Vows"

$\mathcal{E}$ valuating choices and being able to compromise indicates maturity. The sweet oil of compromise lubricates relationships, enabling us to live in harmony and community. We cannot have it our way all the time; giving way graciously can help us reach a greater good than our own happiness.

Yet many women compromise too much, giving in until they no longer know what they stand for or what they want. Compromising our essential selves is a mistake, no matter for whose sake we do it. Our bodies protest when we compromise too much; we get headaches and rashes, suffer from depression, bloat up or waste away, endure insomnia or are constantly sleepy. When compromise causes us to relinquish our authenticity, it's wrong.

I can compromise, but I trust my body to keep
me from compromising too much.

Faith

"Faith is for that which lies on the other side of reason. Faith is what makes life bearable. . . ."

Madeleine L'Engle, *Walking on Water*

*W*hether we place our faith in God or our faith in good, we do not necessarily increase in faith as we age. Much in our world causes pessimism; the more we become aware of the suffering and the horrors, the less faith we may have.

Perhaps we need to remind ourselves that although we may go away from God or good, it does not change nor does it recede from us. If we believe what logic cannot support, if we believe in the ultimate goodness of life, then we have faith. And faith will support us through life's inevitable betrayals, sorrows, and tragedies.

I can believe because I can trust.

Being in Control

"She felt creeping upon her the familiar illusion of control. . . ."

Margaret Drabble, "The Reunion"

For many of us, control often has been illusion. Either we thought we were in control until a crisis revealed we were not, or we controlled trivialities. We decided what to eat for dinner, which brand of vitamins to buy, and when to put away the holiday decorations, while others decided where we lived and whether or not we got promoted.

Sometimes we were offered opportunities to take charge that we, too timid or too afraid of the risks and responsibilities, rejected. Perhaps we refused control over the lives of others. Now, however, we know when to take control and when to let go, when we must assume responsibility and when it is acceptable to turn it over, when we can accept the consequences of taking charge and when we cannot.

Sometimes I need to be in charge, and sometimes it's OK to follow.

Expectations

"I wake expectant, hoping to see a new thing."
Annie Dillard, *Pilgrim at Tinker Creek*

To wake each day expecting joy, pleasant surprises, satisfaction, and fulfillment is a wonderful way to live. A therapist asks herself as she meets each new client, "What will I learn from this person?" and she thrives in the profession.

We can be too naive in our expectations; automatically trusting everyone and discarding reasonable caution leads to disillusion. Expecting too much too fast leads to disappointment. Expecting without doing anything to bring about our expectations triggers dissatisfaction. Leaving everything to chance causes frustration. Letting ourselves be controlled by the expectations of others can be disastrous.

But if we are reasonable in our expectations and labor to bring them to fruition, more often than not they will be fulfilled.

Expecting good things often causes good things to happen.

Accepting "No"

> *"She thinks . . . that 'no' is a word the world
> never learned to say to her."*
>
> Alice Walker, "Everyday Use"

*W*hen the world says "no," some of us react with shock. Some shrug, saying "we probably wouldn't like it anyway." Some mouth "that's OK" when it isn't. Some say nothing for fear of uncontrollable rage. Others are silent because of broken hearts; we have become children again, and "no" means we have lost security and love.

Whether the "no" emanates from partner, friend, colleague, employer, or the universe, we can remember that a single "no" answers a single request on a single occasion. "No" does not imply we are "no-thing" or "no-good," destined for universal rejection. The refusal may be impersonal. Or perhaps we worded our request incorrectly. We can begin the acceptance process by asking in a neutral voice why we have been refused and repeating our question and the answer for clarity.

> *When I accept that the answer is sometimes
> "no," I can accept those occasions with more
> grace.*

Family

*"The family as an institution is both
oppressive and protective. . . ."*
Lillian Breslow Rubin, *Worlds of Pain*

*L*iving in family—rearing children, maintaining homes, and preparing meals—provides joy and heartbreak; full, rich days and sleepless nights; creative outlets and mind-numbing monotony. And living in family engenders ambivalent attitudes about our blood connections—sometimes we feel protected by them and sometimes they seem less compassionate than strangers. Sometimes we feel others care about us and will take care of us because we're family, and sometimes we resent being told, "you have to do this; you're family." Although we do not choose our families, we can choose to be close or distant. We may want extended family get-togethers as often as once a week or once a month—or once a year may be too often. We can withdraw into cozy domesticity with our families—or walk out the door and engage ourselves in the world instead.

*I am part of a family—and I am also myself,
an individual who chooses to live in a family—
or not.*

Longing

*"We can never give up longing and wishing
while we are thoroughly alive."*

George Eliot [Mary Anne Evans],
The Mill on the Floss

ometimes when we find ourselves longing for something, we squash those
feelings down. We see ourselves as five-year-olds—dirty,
sticky, barefoot, wearing limp pinafores. We reject our long-
ings as somehow childish. Yet there's nothing wrong with
continuing to hope for pleasant, lovely things as long as we
live. And we can work as hard as we can to achieve what we
long for.

Longing and yearning make us dissatisfied with the status quo, so we try to overcome the obstacles to the fulfillment of our wishes. Longing is not perpetual unhappiness
with what is nor is it perpetual whining for what will never
be. Longing is simultaneously living in the present and
holding in mind the wish for something else.

*To hunger for the beautiful and the good is part
of my human nature.*

Summer

"There had never been such a June. . . . day
followed day in a sequence of temperate
beauty."

Edith Wharton, *Summer*

After the riotous excess of spring, summer brings a calm, productive tranquility, a seasonal mood many of us also experience now in midlife maturity. Reflection ripens in summer's longer days. In the midst of our most productive years is a good time to reflect on life. Languid heat dissolves surface concerns and irritations; air shimmers over green fields; heat glazes the sea. And what of us? Moving slowly in linen and gauze, drinking iced tea, we pause to reflect, evaluate, and analyze our lives to date. Are we happy and content? Is our work valuable? Are our relationships satisfactory, stable, comforting? Is there something we need to change?

Summer flows me to the river of reflection
where I sit myself down and pause for a while.

Exhaustion

> *"I was so drained I felt as if I were staring*
> *through a telescope at the light of a star dead*
> *for a million years."*
> Isabel Allende, "And of Clay Are We Created"

When we ignore our fatigue, perhaps drinking endless cups of coffee to stay unnaturally alert, exhaustion claims us. We've reached dead ends; our gas gauges show less than empty. Unlike sleep, exhaustion neither refreshes nor renews. Exhaustion depletes our reserves and drains our resources. And restoration of our energy comes slowly after exhaustion.

Can any project be so important to make us feel, when we're finished, that we've been dead a million years? Surely not. We must stop when we're fatigued and rest. We can take mini prayer or meditation breaks. We can walk outside at lunchtime. We can go to bed at 6:30 with a book or rental movie and herbal tea—and stay there until 6:30 the next morning.

> *Working or playing to the point of exhaustion*
> *is foolhardy—and I'm no fool.*

Materialism

> *"Destitution and excessive luxury develop apparently the same . . . intensity of struggle for material goods. . . ."*
>
> Alice James, *The Diary*

Maybe at one time we were humans "owning" instead of humans "being," but most of us have given up possession-based identities by now. "Things" and "stuff" need caretaking and cleaning, inventories and insurance, and we just may not be interested in that anymore. We may even take secret pleasure in defying the standards of our neighborhoods and friends; if others drive Mercedes, we may drive pickups or well-used Volvos. When they expand their homes, we may close off unused rooms.

We enjoy quality and comfort and safe transportation and a few beautiful objects. And we will not work overtime to buy a big-screen TV. Or accept a soul-destroying job to buy a vacation house we're too busy or too exhausted to enjoy.

> *Material goods can become burdens; I'm choosing to disencumber myself.*

Patience

*"I am extraordinarily patient, provided I get
my own way in the end."*

Margaret Thatcher, quoted in *Observer*,
4 April 1989

We are aware of two sides of patience. Patience is sometimes the result of powerlessness, oppression, and suffering, a smile forced through quivering lips because there seems to be nothing else to do. We have discarded this demeaning, dehumanizing patience as we have learned our value. Few people today glorify martyrs.

Another patience comes with maturity, the realization that all of our expectations do not have to be met within the hour—or week—or even year. We can wait because we have learned the pleasures of postponing immediate gratification for long-term, permanent results. We can wait for others to come around to our point of view; we don't have to bludgeon them into submission with our truths. This patience satisfies us with its sweetness.

*Patience is kind and tolerant, but it is not
long-suffering.*

Perseverance

"Nothing succeeds well the first time. Persist in your arrangement. . . ."

Elizabeth Stuart Phelps,
"The Angel Over the Right Shoulder"

We midlife women know well the value of perseverance. We know how to stay with something, how to persist when others walk away because the cause is too ambiguous or too difficult or too long in coming.

We persevere with plans and projects by preserving our health and stamina, maintaining cheerful attitudes, listening to our intuition, and keeping our objectives. We do not allow ourselves to be deflected from what we know is right; we refuse to be patted on the head and told to sit quietly in a corner and mind our own business. Women speak up, we shout out, and we get things accomplished—because we persevere.

Through perseverance I can preserve the people and causes I cherish.

Anticipation

"Nothing is so good as it seems beforehand."
George Eliot [Mary Anne Evans],
Silas Marner

We don't agree with Eliot; anticipation makes life more pleasurable. It's not unreasonable to expect productivity and joy, the support and availability of our friends and partners, and appreciation for our work.

We look forward to receiving an A on an exam, a relaxing bubble bath, lunch with a dear friend, a holiday. When experience reminds us that what we anticipate doesn't always happen or is sometimes disappointingly different, we don't become pessimists or cynics. When we feel a little sour, we can find an antidote in listening to children and young people, eyes shining with possibilities, plan their future. We can harken to our inner children and their dreams of happiness and pleasure for us. We can share their expectant glow and find something in our lives to look forward to all our days.

Anticipation is a pleasure I will give myself.

Curiosity

> *"Stronger even than anger is curiosity—*
> *emotional and intellectual curiosity. . . ."*
> Erica Jong, "Blood and Guts: The Tricky
> Problem of Being a Woman Writer in the Late
> 20th Century"

*P*resented with something as a truth, we want to believe, yet we also want to test, stretch, and try it on to see if it fits us and our experience. Not accepting as gospel everything we are told by others, we want to ascertain truth by ourselves. For we know that only when we run a truth through the sieve of our experience, does it become our truth.

Of course we accept some principles without personal experience—the size of the universe, the nature of volcanic activity, how telecommunication really works. But we continue to be curious about truth, reading, figuring out for ourselves whether a rock or a feather dropped from the same height will reach the ground first—and why. Curiosity makes us eager to satisfy it. Curiosity also eases conversation; slip in a simple "I've always wondered if . . ." and notice how quickly most people respond.

Today I will satisfy my curiosity on one
subject.

Making a Garden

"In search of my mother's garden, I found my own."

Alice Walker,
In Search of My Mother's Garden

*C*ultivating a garden can be a metaphor for cultivating our inner life and making it fruitful. My mother, like Alice Walker's, planted a flower garden wherever she lived. I remember moving into the new house where she and my father and sister still live, and facing a desolate wasteland of a "yard"—no plants, no grass, no trees—just a raw scraped patch of rocky-red Oklahoma soil and a few ugly, thorny weeds. Now it is a shady, restful haven with towering sweet gum trees, banks of glossy holly, beds of iris and daisies and hollyhocks and marigolds, my father's tomato and green pepper patch, grassy paths, a bubbling fountain. She works in the garden for hours, watering, weeding, planting—finding peace, finding her God.

I will renew my garden today even if I just repot a plant.

Anniversaries

> *"Anniversary dates will always kick up anxiety,*
> *whether we are aware of them or not."*
>
> Harriet Goldhor Lerner,
> *The Dance of Intimacy*

*D*ream-workers suggest we pay particular attention to dreams around the anniversaries of significant events—births, deaths, moves, weddings, divorces. Harriet Goldhor Lerner says we should become consciously aware of anxiety triggered by anniversaries to prevent ourselves from reacting foolishly.

Perhaps we could honor anniversaries. We could sit quietly on an anniversary date and let ourselves be flooded with memories of the original event. We could consciously decide to reinforce our memories by looking at photographs or journaling, drawing, painting, or sculpting. Or perhaps we're ready to let go of the event: to write down what we wish to release and burn the writing, or dance the memories away, or bathe them away in a ritual of purification.

> *Anniversaries recur yearly, but I am not bound*
> *to remember and honor them in the same way*
> *every year.*

Blessings

"He had a whim
That sunlight carried blessing."

Amy Lowell, "Patterns"

*N*ature blesses us daily; birds bursting into song just as we stroll past, thunderstorms dissolving the dust of drought, clouds melting from a mountain range to reveal snowy peaks, stars pasted against a midnight-blue velvet sky—and sunlight kissing our faces.

We also receive blessings from others—a stranger's unexpected smile, the touch of someone who cares for us, support from a colleague during an argumentative meeting, the love and compassion of other women during a spiritual retreat.

We know when we have been blessed; our breathing deepens and our chests loosen as our hearts expand, and we know that we, too, participate in life's divine dance.

Giving and receiving blessings brings me bliss.

Parenting Adult Children

"You start shucking off your children from the day you give birth."

Anne Tyler. *Breathing Lessons*

*W*hen our children hit their twenties and thirties, we relax. If they've turned out well, we congratulate ourselves, if they haven't, we've let go of our responsibility for their lives. We've done what we could to the best of our abilities; the rest is up to them. Of course, we never stop loving them, and we're still there for them, listening and giving advice—when we're asked. We may see them every day, or we may see them only once or twice a year. Either has to be all right. We've learned to accept and respect their desires and their lifestyles; in exchange, we've been granted intimacy with them.

In midlife we become friends with our children.

Bliss

"I need not sell my soul to buy bliss."
Charlotte Brontë, *Jane Eyre*

Inexplicable joy sometimes floods our hearts, filling us with loving kindness toward all. Luxuriating in happiness, we try to prolong the ecstasy by analyzing it. What causes our joy? Clear sunny skies after days of rain? Vivaldi's *Concerto in D Major* pouring forth from the radio? Anticipating dinner with a dear friend? We don't know—we only know we want it to last forever. But it doesn't. The sun becomes unpleasantly hot, pleas for the annual fund drive replace Vivaldi, and our friend cancels.

Yet we've had that moment of paradise and we want more. Consciously seeking bliss, we can center our lives around doing the things we love. We can minimize the activities we don't enjoy. We can choose our actions based on how they make us feel rather than their results. Refusing to do that which deadens us, we can put ourselves in the path of bliss.

Expect bliss.

Serving Others

> *"If you can't nourish your own soul, you will use 'good deeds' as power over others."*
> Marion Woodman, *Leaving My Father's House*

My husband helped found a men's support group at our church. When I asked about their function, his response intrigued me. "We know one thing," he said firmly. "We're not going to be like a women's circle."

"Oh," I said, "how's that?"

"Well, we're not going to serve and clean up church dinners. If we're busy doing good deeds all the time, how can we help each other?"

Exactly. As women we spend many hours performing good works, sometimes to the exclusion of listening to others. And we often suffer spiritual bankruptcy—all those assets pouring out and nothing coming in. We may even become resentful; why don't our good works ever benefit us? Sometimes we can relieve this barrenness only by taking some time off to fulfill ourselves, knowing that in time, we will serve others again from full hearts.

Service to others can be valuable when I also nourish myself.

Freedom

*"But most often, particularly with the support
of other women, the coming of age portends
all the freedoms men have always known and
women never. . . ."*
    Carolyn G. Heilbrun, *Writing a Woman's Life*

At fifty we celebrate freedom
        from external standards,
from the demands of femininity,
from the expectations of others,
from prohibitions based only on our gender,
from living only to fulfill the needs of others.
And freedom
    to fail,
    to please ourselves,
    to enjoy the company and support of other women,
    to choose our careers, our partners, and our life
        paths,
    to live the fullest, richest lives we can,
    to protect those we love,
    to be ourselves.

My Creator made me free.

Creativity

*"Creative work is essential to one's well-being
and does not belong to ambition or drive. By
creative work I mean delivering one's own
personal message. . . ."*

Jane Hollister Wheelwright,
For Women Growing Older

*C*reativity is what we do with what we
have. Our creativity expresses our
individuality; it delivers our unique message as no one else
can possibly do. One of the most joyful aspects of turning
fifty is having freedom and time to express our creativity
fully, to develop and harvest talents we had only enough
time to experiment with earlier. No longer as self-conscious
or afraid of failure as when we were younger, we stand
poised on the peak of our experience, ready both to polish
previous gifts and to explore new territory. We follow explorers
like Margaret Mead, doing fieldwork in her seventies,
and Isak Dinesen, whose first book wasn't published until
she was forty-nine.

*I will let my creative juices overflow, watering
and nourishing the seeds of promise within me.*

Higher Power

"Do I now believe, or am I even willing to believe, that there is a Power greater than myself?"

Alcoholics Anonymous

ost of us would answer "yes." Whether we locate the higher power "out there"—beyond ourselves in the heavens or in nature—or within ourselves, our souls reverberate with awareness of something else involving itself in our lives. Perhaps the power within is simply our individual awareness of the power without, our share in the universal divine.

We yearn for oneness with this source of love, creation, and regeneration. When we lose the connection, we lose the capacity to manage our own lives. We feel an aching emptiness that we may try to fill with addictions, busyness, and overwork. Yet all along the higher power is there, waiting for us to come to ourselves, quit the frantic dog-paddling, flip onto our backs, and float in the sunshine.

I'm thankful I can rely on a greater power and don't have to do everything by myself.

Commitment

*"My dream is for everyone . . . to be
committed to something, someone. . . ."*
Denise Chávez, *Face of an Angel*

To be committed wholeheartedly to goals, projects, relationships, or personal growth involves risks. We risk failure, alienation, refusal, and misunderstanding. Yet without commitment, we won't seize opportunities; we might become inert, turning control of our destinies over to others or passively awaiting the turn of fortune's wheel.

We're too old for waiting. We want to commit ourselves and march onward. When we do, we find obstacles we once feared would bar our progress dissolving as we approach. Once we commit, choices narrow and other decisions become simple. We—and others—know what we stand for; our lives begin to loosen and flow, freed from the congealing forces of inaction.

*I commit myself now to action on behalf of
those activities and people I consider most
worthwhile.*

Necessity

"My mother has told me . . . the useful parts.
She will add nothing unless powered by
Necessity, a riverbank that guides her life."

Maxine Hong Kingston,
The Woman Warrior

We no longer allow ourselves to be as governed by necessity as we may have earlier. We still perform some actions because we consider them necessary and essential, but we don't permit necessity to narrow and restrict our creative flow like a riverbank. When it begins to do so, we bring on a spring flood to overflow and even obliterate the riverbank. We list those things we have labeled as necessity, and then we cut those lists in half. We check the extent to which necessity controls our relationships with others. When we find ourselves acting only from duty, then we allow ourselves to spill over that riverbank again with tenderness and compassion and love.

*Necessity can be stern, rigid, narrow, joyless,
and constricted. I must soften it with my
humanity.*

Divorce

"It occurred to her that when . . . [her husband] hadn't been bad company, he'd been no company at all to her."

Tess Gallagher, "Bad Company"

Whether divorce dissolves a short-term partnership or severs a thirty-year marriage, it hurts. No matter how valid the reasons, we may torment ourselves with useless speculation. Instead, we could give ourselves ample time to grieve what was and what might have been. We could connect with the support we have been offered. We could expect less of ourselves, cutting back on activities and conserving our energy. We could seek therapy to understand what happened and what role we played.

We can tell ourselves that couples married at twenty who become totally different people by fifty can hardly expect their marriages to remain the same. We can honor and acknowledge our marriages as integral parts of our past lives, and then we can let go and move on.

Divorce brings sorrow and opportunity for growth and change.

Mindfulness

"There is ecstasy in paying attention. . . . You
see in everything the essence of holiness. . . ."
Anne Lamott, *Bird by Bird*

*M*indfulness means being acutely aware of one thing, concentrating on it while ignoring all other sensory stimuli. So, practicing yoga, we breathe and concentrate on the postures, emptying our minds of all other concerns. And while we make our bodies more supple, we also recharge our energy. For we don't realize how much of our energy can dribble away in mental jabbering. When we practice mindfulness, our energy comes surging back.

We come to mindfulness through meditation, deep breathing, and concentration—we can be mindful anywhere. When we drive, we can focus only on the cars and drivers around us. When we read, we turn off the telephone and the television and become absorbed in our books and magazines. When we eat mindfully, concentrating on each flavor, each aroma, each individual bite, we consecrate our meals.

Any activity performed with mindfulness
becomes an act of worship.

Communication

"Talk for us always meant the same thing.
He'd say a few words. I'd say a few back."
Louise Glück, "Terminal Resemblance"

To fully express ourselves, we have to communicate with others, which can be difficult. As John Gray in *Men Are from Mars, Women Are from Venus* and Deborah Tannen in *You Just Don't Understand* have pointed out, men and women communicate differently. Men provide information and solve problems. Women share feelings, cooperate, and reach consensus. Knowing this, we can sensitize ourselves to potential misunderstandings. For example, when women say "I'm sorry," men hear an apology. If we don't intend an apology, if we meant only to express concern, then we must be more specific—"I'm sorry that happened to you."

We can also improve our communication skills by querying others when we're not sure we understand. We can repeat exactly what we heard and let others correct us if necessary. We can learn to listen rather than just to hear.

To communicate effectively I need to understand
how I could be misunderstood—and take
precautions against it.

Grandmothering

"I suddenly realized that through no act of my own I had become biologically related to a new human being."

Margaret Mead, *Blackberry Winter*

ecause we are not responsible for becoming grandmothers, our grandchildren provide undiluted pleasure. We care for them and nurture them and stand in for their parents when necessary and when we can. And, at the end of the day, weekend, or week, we return to our absorbing work and interests, our peaceful adult houses, our childless lives.

Being around young children offers us the opportunity to redeem any mistakes we may think we made in rearing our children. We can read shelves of books to them. We can faithfully attend soccer games and dance recitals. Our egos do not depend on having them reflect us, so we don't have to form these grand children into our images. We let them be themselves. We support them and love them so unequivocally that they come to us out of love, not obligation.

Grandchildren are the bonus of motherhood.

Courage

"Courage is a willingness to act from the heart . . . not knowing what will be required of you next. . . ."

Jean Shinoda Bolen *Gods in Everyman*

Sometimes we envision courage as warrior action—fighting medieval dragons or Hitler's army—or heroic deeds—dramatic rescues at sea or from fire. But living a woman's life has always required courage—maintaining autonomy in our relationships, leaving family and friends to travel across countries and continents, risking life to give birth to another.

Some days it takes courage to get up; we don't know what will be required of us this day, and we fear being unable to do it. But we gather our thoughts, utter a hasty prayer for guidance, and follow our hearts. And somehow we do get through the day, realizing even some success—solutions to perpetual parking problems, confrontations resolved amicably and honestly, rumors traced to their source and corrected.

Help me recognize and appreciate the small acts of courage we women carry out every day.

Disabilities

> *"Those of us who are disabled are continual reminders of nature's random workings. I prefer to think of those who are not disabled as* temporarily *able-bodied."*
>
> Amber Coverdale Sumrall,
> "Crossing the High Country"

$\mathcal{S}$ome of us live with handicaps or disabilities now; others may face them later. What will we make of them? Disabilities constantly remind us that our corporal bodies include the incorporeal; we are both body and soul. Women who live energetically and courageously and fully despite handicapped bodies exemplify this. Barbara Jordan, crippled by multiple sclerosis, continued to serve her community and her country until her death. Vassar Miller, former poet laureate of Texas, writes beautiful verse and struggles with cerebral palsy. We all know women who daily battle infirmities of body, mind, and spirit—and succeed. Perhaps they find their disabilities not limiting but expansive.

> *If I become disabled, may I too be granted the courage and grace to live the fullest life of which I am capable.*

Companionship

*"After we came in we sate in deep silence at
the window—I on a chair and William with
his hand on my shoulder. We were deep in
Silence and Love, a blessed hour."*
Dorothy Wordsworth, *The Grasmere Journals*

*C*ompanionship varies in intensity
from the deep relationship Dorothy
Wordsworth describes with her brother William to our relationships with people with whom we share an interest, enjoying their company while engaged in the activity, but not especially or particularly at other times.

I'm a faithful student of yoga, attending class at the same studio several times a week. I have companions there, people whom I'm always glad to see at a practice, people whose presence enriches my participation, and yet I don't even know most of their last names. We meet only to study yoga. Most of us have companions of this type—people with whom we share early morning jogging or gourmet dinners or books. Most activities become more pleasurable when shared with others; we welcome companions into our lives.

*I have room in my life for companions and
being companionable.*

Judgment/Criticism

"Surviving judgment, like admitting love, takes courage."

Marianne Wiggins, "Grocer's Daughter"

As autonomous women, sure of our identities, confident of our place in the universe, and unafraid of speaking our truths, we inevitably face judgment, criticism, censorship, and outright condemnation. We know we will, and we continue speaking from our hearts because we must. But sometimes the negative responses burden us.

It may help to ask those who are judging or criticizing us simply to tell us how they feel. Then we can accept the responsibility for causing those feelings—or not. Sometimes their criticism turns out not to have anything to do with us. Sometimes it does. We cannot live authentically without occasionally hurting others and even betraying them. Maintaining our identities and operating from our truth can be painful and difficult. But in our maturity, we accept criticism and continue to do and say what we feel is right.

Give me the judgment to evaluate criticism and respond to it while maintaining my own integrity.

Conscious Living

> *"Consciousness itself does not hinder living in the present. In fact, it is only to a heightened awareness that the great door to the present opens at all."*
>
> Annie Dillard, *Pilgrim at Tinker Creek*

*B*eing present to the moment means using our senses instead of our heads, to be acutely aware of savoring a plump dewy strawberry, inhaling the perfume of a rose, watching the first star emerge in the dusk, and cradling a baby's delicate head.

Living consciously, we live each day intensely. Dropping the heavy cloaks that shield us from sensory overload, we really experience our lives. If we find that too much to bear, then perhaps we should consider simplifying our surroundings. Eating consciously, we eat more sensibly and more healthily. Watching television consciously, we watch less of it. Living our friendships and relationships consciously, we may have fewer of them—but they nourish and fulfill us.

I would like to live more consciously and less from habit and custom.

Manners

> *"Good manners and tolerance . . . can often transform disaster into good fortune."*
>
> Maya Angelou,
> *Wouldn't Take Nothing for My Journey Now*

We probably learned our manners from our mothers; women seem to be the custodians of small courtesies whose importance must not be minimized. Perhaps our friends don't really need to write a thank-you note after dinner at our home, but don't we glow when we get them? Perhaps we don't have to make an effort to bring a shy person into a general conversation, but aren't we rewarded when that person sparkles at being included? Perhaps we don't have to smile sympathetically at service personnel, but aren't we happy when they give us a grateful glance?

It's also good manners not to impose our will on others, but to leave decisions open for agreement or disagreement, except when that courtesy would be destructive—not telling the truth when we are asked point-blank; letting our partner drive drunk rather than hurt his feelings by demanding the keys.

Although it's sometimes tricky, I will manage to be both courteous and honest.

Conformity/Nonconformity

"At a very early period she had apprehended
instinctively the dual life—that outward existence
which conforms, the inward life which questions."
Kate Chopin, *The Awakening*

In our desire for acceptability and intimacy, we have all been affected by the duality of conformity/nonconformity. Outwardly we maintain the personae we assume everyone expects while inwardly we seethe, longing, as Emily Dickinson once wrote, to burst "all the doors" and dance "like a Bomb."

Because we value our independence and self-sufficiency, we must at times dance to our inner music, not to the drumbeats of the marching band everyone else hears. Witnessing our free-flowing dances, our freedom of self-expression will encourage our younger sisters to join us. Together we will change society's notion of conformity for women. And later in life, we may find ourselves "conforming" to these new standards when we haven't changed our nonconformity at all.

There are times when I must conform to societal
expectations and times when I must be myself.

Identity

*"She was back again in the freedom of her
own identity . . . with all the strength of her
maturity to savour its joy."*

Dorothy Richardson, "The Ordeal"

*W*e have never been so clear about who and what we are as we are now. We have at last come into our own. We have the maturity and knowledge to seek and appreciate whatever helps us maintain our identities. Free from the most burdensome domestic work, we lead the lives we have always wanted for ourselves—useful, purposeful lives, lives neither circumscribed by our sex nor mandated by others.

No longer do we sneak peeks in every mirror and shop window we pass to make certain a flesh-and-blood woman strides down the sidewalk or through the store. Minds, bodies, emotions, and spirits united at last, we are certain of our existence.

*No longer primarily identified by relationships
or occupations, I am now simply myself.*

Responsibility

> *"Responsibility, no matter how difficult or painful, was what gave my life depth and meaning and resonance. . . ."*
>
> Ingrid Bengis, "The Middle Period"

We come to our age willing to assume responsibility for our decisions and to accept the consequences of our actions. At the same time, we refuse responsibility that does not belong to us. When our companions run late, we remove ourselves from the consequences of tardiness by going on alone. When our families fight, we avoid mediating their quarrels. When our adult children agonize over decisions, we point out pros and cons *if we're asked*, but we allow them the privilege of taking responsibility for their decisions.

Having made our own choices and accepted the responsibility rightfully ours, we move on, for the burden of responsibility is felt less when moving than when standing still.

I am responsible for my own choices and actions and no one else's.

Keeping Rules/
Breaking Rules

"It is not the rightness that makes keeping the rules so appealing to us; it is the safeness."

Jean Benedict Raffa,
The Bridge to Wholeness

Obeying rules we believe in, rules such as stopping at red lights and avoiding drinking and driving, rules that make our communities safe and orderly, is fine. But we may keep other rules not because they're right, but because they make us feel conventional and "safe." We need to question those rules and even break them, especially the ones governing women's behavior. For example, how many of us grew up believing that women should never be assertive or that self-sacrifice made us more "womanly"—rules that we now break with impunity?

Rules that circumscribe professions by gender, preventing, for example, women from officiating in religious positions, may need to be broken as a signal they need to be changed.

Obeying rules may keep me "safe," but I choose to rebel against unjust rules.

Contemplation

*"This Power of Contemplation and
Reflection . . . chiefly distinguishes the
Human from the Brute Creation. . . ."*
Eliza Haywood, *The Female Spectator*

We reflect and contemplate more now than when we were younger. When things occur, we have a wealth of knowledge based on previous experience to serve us. We no longer assume that our first thoughts or solutions are correct. We do not apologize for hesitating to make snap judgments.

Because we are more content with ourselves, we do not flee our interior life; we welcome opportunities to reflect on problems, viewing them now from this perspective, now from that, looking ahead to the long-range effects of solutions.

Contemplation serves more than problem solving. We ponder our place in the starry universe—and in our nuclear families. We reflect on the goals we've set ourselves—are they realistic or do they need some modification? We contemplate our futures—how do we want to live five years from now?

*Contemplation richly rewards me for living a
full life.*

Discipline

"Self-discipline is something you consciously devise to help you order your life and achieve certain goals."

Helen DeRosi, *Women and Anxiety*

*D*iscipline and spontaneity coexist. Order and schedules and goals deserve our attention—and so do disorder, flexibility, and change. Perhaps we practice self-discipline most of the time in most areas of our lives—and relish the freedom to abandon it some of the time. I prefer the public and shared areas of our house to be tidy, but my study usually overflows with clutter, love seat heaped with open books, shelves submerged beneath my sacred objects, computer table covered with folders, desk heaped with textbooks and student papers. But I know where to find everything. And I keep my door shut.

We choose discipline; we practice it to reach the goals we have set for ourselves. Discipline should be flexible, an outline rather than *the* authoritative textbook.

Discipline provides a good map for my life's journey, but I will not let it become the complete itinerary.

Childlessness

> *"There is much wisdom, much foresight in my*
> *will not to be a mother."*
>
> Alexandra David-Neel, letter in Olga Kenyon,
> *800 Years of Women's Letters*

*I*n 1905 Alexandra David-Neel, the Tibetan explorer, carefully explained why she had chosen to be childless, a sentiment echoed by many of us. Gloria Steinem, for example, has said she didn't want children because of the social inequalities of mothering in America and has never missed them.

Who we are now does not depend on whether or not we have given birth; lives that do not revolve around children are purposeful, rewarding, and whole. We find our passion in creativity, work, friends, and relationships. If we sometimes yearn for the company of children, we can indulge our young relatives or godchildren or volunteer to work with children. Children can make us immortal, but so can work and contributions to the larger community.

There is more to my life as a woman than
reproduction.

Self-Control

"It was something I was good at: sitting still,
    not moving.
I did it to be good. . . ."

Louise Glück, "Appearances"

Sitting motionless and shutting down our emotions were perhaps the only ways we could control ourselves as youngsters. Now we practice self-control differently. We know when we must restrict our behavior and when we don't have to. We might like to respond in kind to a motorist who cuts us off, but we don't because it isn't safe—he may have a gun on the seat beside him. We feel like venting our anger at a flight attendant for the policies of her airline, but we don't because she's not the appropriate person.

Self-control doesn't mean denial; it means managing our actions and our feelings in terms of goals and strategies we set—I won't sleep until noon on Saturday because my body doesn't need it and because I want the time to do something else.

Self-control helps me reach my goals.

Selfish or Selfless?

*"There were almost no women . . . who were
not actively and obsessively preoccupied with
a choice between self and other. . . ."*

Mary Field Belenky *et al.*,
Women's Ways of Knowing

Women absorbed in self-development at some point usually question themselves: "Am I being selfish? Shouldn't I be using this time to do something for others?"

We each must answer for ourselves. I can only describe what I did. Beginning at fifty, I spent four years in intensive self-examination, giving up volunteer work, withdrawing from some activities and friendships, cutting back on teaching hours. By detaching myself, I could see myself and my participation more clearly. I learned that demanding time for myself and saying no was not selfish but essential. I learned the difference between genuine compassion and pseudocompassion that served to distract me from my own issues. And then I could return to affinity and service.

*Living authentically, I cycle through selfishness
and selflessness.*

Connectedness

> *"Women . . . are searching for and finding their connectedness."*
>
> Sherry Ruth Anderson and Patricia Hopkins,
> *The Feminine Face of God*

We yearn to be connected to something outside ourselves—causes, relationships, nature, our higher power—yet we also want to maintain our individuality within those connections. Women value attachment so greatly that sometimes we sacrifice ourselves to become "we" instead of "I." To maintain healthy connections and independence simultaneously, we must keep a sense of our identities intact.

We can dissolve into the beauties of nature for a time, feeling one with a landscape. But eventually we wake and realize our human identity; we connect with dawn and squirrels and spring rain, but we are not they. During meditation and prayer, we refresh and replenish our spirituality by connecting with our higher power, but not to the extent that we abandon our daily responsibilities and human connections.

It's good to feel a part of—and it's good to feel apart from.

Secrecy

*"But after a year and a half the champagne of
secrecy had gone flat."*

Rona Jaffe, "Rima the Bird Girl"

*M*aturity teaches us when maintaining
secrecy is wise and powerful and
when maintaining secrecy is weakening and self-destructive.
Neither as open as Generation X-ers, nor as reticent as our
parents, we maintain a nice balance on secrecy. Carrying a
few secrets in our hearts, telling less than we know, acting
mysterious at times, is delicious. Maintaining a core of
inner privacy—those things we would never willingly
reveal—is necessary for our souls. We never know how others
may respond to our heart-truths; our revelations may
wither and die under the wrong response.

But when truth must be spoken, when secrets closeted
too long in the dark must be dragged out and exposed to the
light, we can do that, too.

*I know what secrets it is life-preserving to
keep —and what secrets it is life-preserving to
reveal.*

Success

"Once you do achieve number one, you don't relax and enjoy it."

Billie Jean King, *Billy Jean*

*M*any of us find relaxing and enjoying success difficult. Once we've tasted that ambrosia, we want to feast on it every day, yet we find becoming successful easier than staying successful. Our interior judge speaks up, "Well, if *you* accomplished that, it must not have been that difficult." So we set more difficult goals. We can run a ten-minute mile, so why not a nine-minute? Our promotion came with a salary increase to $60,000—why not aim for $75,000 next year?

Perhaps we can escape the trap of setting ever more difficult individual goals by rethinking success as less individualistic and more communal. In the film *Mr. Holland's Opus*, the protagonist discovers at retirement that the success he had sought and failed to achieve as a composer had been realized in the contributions he had made to the successes of his students.

Success is sweetest when shared.

Exercise

"I wish to persuade women to endeavour to
acquire strength, both of mind and body. . . ."
Mary Wollstonecraft,
A Vindication Concerning the Rights of Women

We believe in the mind/body connection, so it makes sense to exercise our bodies as well as our minds. Exercise brings both strength and flexibility. Exercise relieves crankiness, anxiety, and depression by releasing endorphins, a natural "high," into the bloodstream. At the end of a trying, weary day, how nice it is to practice yoga, walk through the park on the way home, work out at a health club, or dance ourselves sweaty. How much better we feel afterward—relaxed and renewed, restored to better spirits.

If we don't habitually exercise, we can start now by finding a physical activity we enjoy, being realistic about our potential, maintaining a regular schedule, being clear about our objectives, and, if it helps, persuading someone to participate with us.

Being physically fit keeps me emotionally and
mentally fit.

Conscience

"If all the world hated you, and believed you wicked, while your own conscience approved you, and absolved you from guilt, you would not be without friends."

Charlotte Brontë, *Jane Eyre*

Whether we call our inner truth conscience, higher power, God- or Goddess-within, or soul, we recognize it as our best and truest self. Conscience is not an external voice we've internalized; neither does it cause guilt. Just the opposite. Guilt comes when we act against our inner authority. Conscience guides us home to ourselves, saying "no thanks" to the second or third glass of wine, closing our lips when we would repeat a malicious rumor, walking us away from a casual but dangerous flirtation. Conscience sometimes conforms to societal standards; sometimes it does not. When we speak our truths, we must at times argue against conventional truths.

Realizing I have not compromised my conscience in words or actions brings me peace at day's end.

Marriage

> *"I think that my natural vocation is marriage.*
> *I like to be with one person, to share secrets*
> *with him; I like to sleep in the same bed with*
> *the man I love."*
>
> Isabel Allende, quoted in Cathleen Rountree,
> *On Women Turning Fifty*

*M*idlife is a good time to remember why so many of us chose to marry and stay married. Perhaps we wanted an empathetic listener or someone to share experiences. Perhaps we wanted to create and maintain a family. Perhaps we yearned for completion and fulfillment as part of a pair. Certainly marriage provides a safe environment for revealing our most private needs, and expecting they will be considered valid.

Marriage is a living organism that must be nurtured by creating time for each other. Talking openly and often about our inner and outer lives. Laughing together. Sharing a vision for our future. Apologizing when we're wrong and forgiving when we've been wronged.

> *Marriage does not destroy individuality; it*
> *contains and protects it.*

Destiny

> *"'The only way to escape one's destiny is to
> enjoy it. I will stay here.'"*
>
> Emily Prager, "A Visit from the Footbinder"

*I*s accepting our destiny fatalistic or realistic? How do we distinguish between our natural destinies and the destinies others may have imposed on us? In the story quoted above, a little Chinese girl accepts as her destiny the torture of foot-binding to attract the "right" husband. We would disagree. We "enjoy" individual rather than societal destiny, non-conformity rather than conformity.

If at times we must accept what life brings us, we work within those patterns to remain authentic. Surrounded by petty jealousy and squabbles, we can be compassionate and loving. Surrounded by prejudice, we can be open-minded. Surrounded by greed, we can be generous.

I can choose how to accept my destiny.

Looking Fifty

"As a matter of principle, I declare I will never dye gray out of my hair, wear blue contact lenses on my brown eyes, or buy clothes that feel terrible just because they're in style."

Anndee Hochman,
"What I Know from Noses"

Fifty looks like us: petite and queenly tall, slim and full-figured, brunette curls and intricate gray braids, power suits and flowing silk, smooth faces and wear-wrinkles, marathon runners and mile-a-day walkers. When we accept ourselves at fifty, we don't respond to "You're fifty? You don't look fifty" with blushes of pleasure. Instead, we say, *"This is* what fifty looks like because I'm fifty and this is how I look." If twenty-five is silver, fifty is gold—rust-free, gleaming, powerful, perfect.

Accepting our appearance, we also fight to correct ageist stereotypes of older women. The women in their seventies we see participating in aerobics and Senior Olympics, hiking in the mountains, and swimming laps have glowing, vital, healthy bodies and faces. They are beautiful.

I am proud to be fifty and look my age.

Hesitation

"She would always look anyone in the eye.
Hesitation was no part of her nature."
Alice Walker, "Everyday Use"

We're certainly more fearless now than before. Confidence comes with age and experience just as surely as wisdom. We don't hang our heads to avoid meeting the eyes of others. We don't hang behind or on our partners in social situations. We don't hesitate to speak up when we are treated discourteously and when we have been wronged.

We distinguish between shrinking timidity, prudent hesitation, and reckless abandon. We know when to leap and when to linger, when to volunteer and when to sit on our hands, when to confront and when to avoid conflict. We know when to advance ourselves and our causes and when to leave the promotion to others.

I hesitate long enough to evaluate situations
and people, then I move forward—or away.

Changing Residences

> *"Moving is a lot like making love: You hope for*
> *satisfaction when it's over . . . [and]*
> *experience is worth more than advice."*
>
> Frances Weaver, *Midlife Musings*

In transition at fifty, we may find ourselves changing residences again. Whether for the first time—or the seventeenth—moving house can be painful and difficult. However, we can use the opportunity to clear out debris—graduate school notes, unread books, decorative objects that no longer appeal, dated clothes and furniture. We can return to the children the beer-can, coin, and sports-cards collections, cheerleader uniforms, dried corsages, and wedding dresses.

Then we can grieve the homes we leave, the storehouses of our memories—family rooms where we celebrated and fought, joked and cried; bedrooms where we frolicked and nursed others through illness; studies where we worked, dreamed, wrote and painted; gardens we cultivated through the seasons.

> *A woman connects to home deeply and sacredly;*
> *I will honor the mourning that accompanies my*
> *moves.*

Choices

> "My feet choose the way, and every step, every
> choice is an exclusion of possibility, a
> diminution of the boundless self."
>
> Joan Connor, "Broken Vows"

Actually, as we mature and see things whole, we don't see choice as this limiting. We begin to see that most choices are neither irrevocable nor exclusive. We can change our minds and our life paths. Our world changes rapidly, and we know we must be flexible and open to other options. When we choose one path, we also must be able to backtrack if necessary, to feel free to explore interesting side paths, and even to take long detours. To choose one thing does mean another must be excluded—but only for the time being, not necessarily forever. To choose to be tender, for example, does not mean that we cannot also be firm when a situation demands it.

Choice helps me narrow and focus; it does not have to be exclusive.

Optimism

*"I do not believe that true optimism can come
about except through tragedy."*
Madeleine L'Engle, *Two-Part Invention*

Optimism came easily for most of us
as children, innocent and inexperi-
enced, finding the world and all its inhabitants good. However, this childish optimism dissolved as we matured and
discovered the reality of the tooth fairy, the Easter bunny,
and Santa Claus.

Mature optimism, the optimism we now experience, is
deeper, wiser—and Teflon-coated. We know evil exists, and
we know some people are motivated by hatred and cruelty.
We know miracles do not always occur when we pray for
them. We have been brushed—and crushed—by tragedy.
And yet . . . we arise each morning expecting good things
to happen, that those we encounter will be friendly and
well-meaning, and that our work, performed thoughtfully
and responsibly, will turn out well.

*I'm not a "cockeyed optimist"; I see life
clearly—and I find reasons to rejoice.*

Wholeness

"There is a whole of which one is a part,
and . . . in being a part one is whole."
Ursula K. Le Guin, *The Lathe of Heaven*

The wholeness we either experience or yearn for now is a perfect accord between our conscious and unconscious selves. We seek the total integration of our minds, bodies, emotions, and spirits, complete acceptance of all our parts, light and shadow, playful child and fierce Amazon.

In wholeness, we realize our connection to the earth; we know that we breathe in unison with all other living organisms. We recognize that the universe itself constantly strives to bring about this harmonious union, blending incongruities, discord, and disparate parts into a perfect whole. So, too, we extend the wholeness we have achieved to our culture and our society, healing all that is wounded and broken.

The circle — containing all, excluding
nothing — symbolizes wholeness. Breathing and
expanding, living, moving, containing my own
contrarieties, I also am whole.

Trust

"No amount of therapy or analysis can heal a heart that cannot trust."

Marion Woodman, *The Pregnant Virgin*

*T*rusting ourselves: accepting our nature without suppression or judgment. Exercising our abilities without comparison or denigration. Choosing wisely for ourselves and others. When we trust ourselves, we remember how often we make correct assessments, what good qualities we have, and how talented we are.

Trusting others: believing that those to whom we reveal vulnerability will support and comfort us, respecting our secrets and our privacy, honoring our thoughts and actions. When we have trouble trusting others because we have been betrayed too often, we can begin to heal ourselves by trusting someone with a small matter. As a spider spins her web one fragile silken strand across the abyss and then another and then another, we expand our trust as we feel more confident.

No rock can destroy my web of trust; I can reweave it.

Pride

"Pride was what kept you from admitting you had any problems, even when everybody knew you did."

Jane Smiley, *Moo*

At our age, we've learned how tricky pride can be. We know the glory of taking pride in accomplishment, success, and victory—and we know the damage of letting pride in past achievements prevent us from seeking help with present problems. We know the glory of taking pride in the successes of our friends, colleagues, partners, and children for their sakes— and the damage of taking pride because of what we think we contributed to those successes.

We've also learned the difference between rightful pride based on our solid achievements and puffed-up pride that depends on putting down others. We recognize that taking pride in accidents of birth, strokes of luck, fortuitous circumstances, and the right friends is false pride that can only serve to isolate us from others.

I can take pride in my genuine achievements without being proud.

Stillness/Silence

"'How still, how happy!'"
Emily Brontë, "How Still, How Happy!"

O̶ur world tends to equate productivity and noise, but many glorious events happen in silence—grass and grandchildren, embryos and elephants grow; water seeks the sea; planets rotate in their cycles. We must reclaim silence and stillness for ourselves, for if we lack privacy in our workplaces and in our homes, silence can replace physical space. We can periodically withdraw into stillness, silencing radios, TVs, CD players, and telephones to achieve a sense of solitude in which we hear only our breathing and our pulses. We can also seek that stillness in nature, walking or watching unobserved, quietly listening. When we achieve inner tranquility, we reflect that peaceful stillness and offer others a share in our salvation.

Stillness is a soul-need, as essential as the murmur of companionship.

Widowhood

*"It's her only hope, the wish to move
backwards."*

Louise Glück, "A Fantasy"

The poet describes early widowhood when we long for the days when he lived. We feel pain so sharp, so overpowering that we wonder how we can get out of bed, how we can continue our lives. He who would have taken away the pain with hugs and comfort is dead. We feel anger—how dare he do this to me? Why didn't he take better care of his health?—and then our anger shames us.

Our grief is recursive, but bit by bit it begins to recede. We find solace in faith, the solicitude of friends and family, and nature. We don't "get over it" or "through it"; we absorb the fact of our widowhood and its attendant emotions. They become part of us without controlling every action, thought, and emotion. We can remember our lives together and find joy.

*I accept the pain of widowhood as I accepted the
joy of being a wife.*

Recovery

"It is never too late to recover, and, no matter
what our age, we have all the time we need."
Helen Larimore, Olde Women in Recovery

ecovery involves living consciously,
accepting our feelings, and meeting
our needs without causing pain to others or ourselves. Many
of us are in recovery now and perhaps others need to consider recovering from societal oppression that devalues us
for our sex or our age. We may need to recover from
abuse—financial, emotional, sexual—dysfunctional families, and addictions—overspending, overeating, sex, alcohol, prescription or narcotic drugs.

We have time to recover and many resources: self-help
books, self-examination, support groups, and therapy. We
can use prayer and meditation to recover ourselves. We can
open ourselves to others in recovery and share our stories.

*Recovery is not a goal but a process, a process I
can begin today by choosing to acknowledge one
self-destructive habit or negative emotion.*

Gardening

"The garden is growth and change and that means loss as well as constant new treasures to make up for a few disasters."

May Sarton, *Journal of a Solitude*

Gardening provides a marvelous release for many of us. Nourishing the earth, getting dirt under our nails, pulling weeds, staking plants, and planting seeds and bulbs nourishes us, too. Gardening provides clarity. In a garden seeds are planted, grow, bud, blossom, and fade. Some succumb to insects and heat; others thrive. Some expensive nursery plants never live up to their potential, while a humble cutting shared by a neighbor sturdily blooms year after year. The gaudy hibiscus has no scent and dies in a day; the inconspicuous lily of the valley perfumes its presence. A hard freeze in December turns the radiant glory of cyclamens to mush; a heat wave in October wilts the newly planted pansies. Growth, change, loss, disasters, and splendid surprises—a garden models life itself.

Gardening reminds me nothing is permanent, and change brings both loss and redemption.

Worry

"*She had never realized before that worry could be dumped in someone else's lap like a physical object. She should have done it years ago.*"

Anne Tyler, *Ladder of Years*

We haven't lived to be fifty without worry. But now we worry less because we know we can't control everything, and we'll never make everybody happy. We don't worry about the future so much because we've accepted our mortality. We'd rather live full lives now than worry about what might happen if we . . . go backpacking in the Sierra Nevadas, sign up for college, change jobs, dump unresponsive partners, move to a maintenance-free condominium, tell our children to raise their own children. So we go ahead and do it.

What, after all, has worry ever given us except seamed foreheads and sad eyes? It never postpones conflict or calamity, so it doesn't deserve an altar in our hearts.

Worry doesn't anchor; it crushes.

Virtue

*"Elegance is inferior to virtue. . . . The first
object of laudable ambition is to obtain a
character as a human being. . . ."*

Mary Wollstonecraft, *A Vindication
Concerning the Rights of Women*

The definition of a virtuous woman as
one who preserves her chastity before
marriage and practices sexual faithfulness afterward may
strike us as quaint. But as women today we continue to
practice the virtues of spirituality, peacefulness, nurtur-
ance, compassion, responsibility, honesty, and loyalty. We
embody these virtues because we freely choose them by listening to our hearts, not because others have preached what
we must do. We speak the truth because we have found
deception soul-destroying. We seek peace because enmity
upsets our harmony. We act responsibly because we prefer
living in a society in which everyone practices responsibility. We show compassion because we live in community, and
the pain of others affects our well-being. We demonstrate
loyalty because we want to trust—and be trustworthy.

I am a virtuous woman; I walk my talk.

Social Justice

"She feels as if . . . all the needs of protesting
women of whom she has read with a vague
displeasure have come home to her."
George Egerton [Mary Chavelita Dunne],
"Virgin Soil"

As we sift through our concerns and our causes, we begin to let some go while becoming even more passionate about others. Many of us are passionate now about social justice because the need is overwhelming, particularly for women and children. Daily the news documents the problem: continuing inequities in pay scales and employment opportunities, soaring numbers of children living below the poverty level, increasing acts of violence against women, and harsh attacks on female politicians.

We can take courage from the efforts of other women. At a workshop a marvelous woman in her seventies spoke about her efforts to humanize women's prisons. "It's wonderful," she said, "to be my age. Nobody realizes what I'm doing until after I've accomplished everything I want to do."

Never underestimate the power of women for good.

Reticence

"I know the lure of reticence,
need masked as silent mystery,
hiding a dark side."
　　Hallie Moore, "Getting Through the Night"

*T*he poet reveals that reticence attracts just as the migrating duck is drawn closer and closer to the unnatural stillness of the decoy. Sometimes we would like to be women of mystery, wearing black with veiled hats. A little reticence, a little mystery may serve us well—there is no need for all our acquaintances to know everything there is to know about us.

But we may practice reticence because we are ashamed of our dark sides, our shadow selves. We may fear others will discover that underneath our wizardry is another woman flawed like themselves. Perhaps we use mystery to disguise our real feelings. If so, we might consider opening ourselves to more intimacy.

Reticence can be a virtue or a vice; I know the difference.

Rebellion

"Rebellion is the desperate assertion of our
value in the face of all that attacks it, the cry
of refusal in the face of control."

Starhawk, *Truth or Dare*

Some of us have rebelled all of our lives. Stubborn little girls, we refused to be polite to people we didn't like or join the conspiracy to hide family secrets. As adolescents hypocrisy and injustice infuriated us. As passionate young women dedicated to causes, we argued, protested, marched. As mothers, we looked for options to the traditional delegation of parenting and domestic responsibilities. And now we continue to rebel against sexist and ageist stereotypes, against societal strictures that prevent our development.

Others of us may only just now feel secure enough in personhood, relationships, and life situations to rebel, to question the opinions of the majority, and to begin refusing to be controlled by the expectations of others.

If I need to rebel to protect my values, my
family, and my community, I can and I will.

Survival

> *"In people to whom 'the worst' has happened,
> [there is] an almost transcendent freedom, for
> they have . . . survived it."*
>
> Carol Pearson, *The Hero Within*

By the time we've reached fifty, many of us have survived abusive childhoods, dysfunctional families, gross injustice in the workplace, or horrible accidents. Sometimes these tragedies were so overwhelming, we could not see the gift of our survival. Yet facing and surviving the worst makes us supple; we will bend rather than break beneath the next blow. Surviving also liberates us, and freedom is power.

Listen to Holocaust survivors describe their lives afterward—how they poured their energies into raising families, exercising creativity, and speaking up for justice and accountability. Listen to the bravery of sexual abuse survivors as they accept themselves and even accept abuse as a gift that helped them become the women they now are.

> *Surviving the worst life offers also frees me to
> accept life's pleasures.*

Acceptance

"There is a sense of order and meaning, . . . a sense of one's own life cycle as something that had to be as it was."

Jean Prétat, *Coming to Age*

oday we accept our physical bodies, our gifts and limitations, and our place in the world. Many of us now also accept the pain and tragedies of our past. All our experiences, good and bad, have contributed to the selves we accept with joy and thanksgiving. We won't waste time in regrets. In science-fiction plots, time travelers usually are warned not to alter or interfere with events in the time to which they journey because even well-meant actions may have disastrous consequences in the future. All that has happened to us has had a hand in our creation. When we accept the women we are, we must also accept the women we were. With such acceptance comes peace and a discovery of the patterns of our lives.

I accept myself now as I accept everything that has happened to me.

Kindness

> *"I had expected her to be cold and cruel. Her*
> *kindness took me by surprise and tears*
> *washed down my face."*
>
> Stephany Brown, "Holy Places"

Kindness costs little and can be practiced anywhere . . . anytime . . . with anyone. Kindness reaches across a chair to touch the arm of another and whisper, "Are you all right?" Kindness pauses to let another motorist enter the freeway. Kindness picks the last two camellias from the bush by the front door to give to the flowerless neighbor. Kindness gets up in the night and brings back a glass of cool water for her restless partner. Kindness eases the tension of a friend with a shoulder and neck massage. Kindness laughs at the punch line even when she's heard the joke before. Kindness buys a rose from the child selling them under the freeway and gives it away before she arrives home. Kindness looks at the pictures of the new grandbaby and says, "she's beautiful"—and means it. Kindness gets up early Sunday morning and brings back fresh bagels.

I can be kind.

Boundaries

*"When people are self-centered, they have no
boundaries and do not know where they end
and others begin."*

Anne Wilson Schaef,
Beyond Therapy, Beyond Science

*M*aturity gives us good boundary sense; we maintain personal boundaries, permitting those we choose access to our innermost feelings without allowing them to pillage. We permit others their boundaries of space and time and privacy; we do not, for example, hound our professional friends for advice during social occasions. We know the difference between friendly concern and prying, and we can hold public figures accountable without insisting on access to the most intimate details of their private lives.

And we also know that boundaries probably need to be periodically evaluated and changed. We, like other living organisms, like institutions, and society itself, are in a state of flux. We can discard our own outdated boundaries.

*I believe in boundaries, both physical and
psychological.*

Nature

> *"In the immensity of the desert the whirl of trivialities . . . all fell away. I was suspended in timelessness—sand, sky, and space. What a relief it was to let go. . . ."*
>
> Anzia Yezierska, "Hester Street"

When we are too much inside climate-controlled buildings with artificial lighting, wearing constrictive clothing and hard shoes, we ache with a vague sense of loss. We should follow our instincts and seek the comfort and restoration of nature, letting a sense of her permanence and timelessness flow over us, purging away the busyness and worries that consume us. Walking barefoot on the grass of our suburban lawn, we ground ourselves in our ancient mother. Sitting under a tree in an urban park, we realize peace. Walking along the shore, we soothe ourselves with the eternal rhythm of the ever-flowing tides. Facing a desert landscape of rippling sand and towering cacti, we acknowledge permanence.

In the timelessness of nature I awaken to myself.

Validation

*"If we can't feel good about our skills and
accomplishments, no one else can, either."*

Christiane Northrup,
Women's Bodies, Women's Wisdom

What a novel idea! Instead of depending on others for validation and self-worth, we can begin with ourselves. The approbation of others that we seek will follow. In a society geared to productivity, sometimes we tend to deprecate our own accomplishments because they seem small—a friendship healed here, a writer encouraged there, a neighborhood park cleaned and restored, some children fed hot breakfasts before school. If no one else honors these accomplishments, we can—in ourselves and in our sisters. We can form our own organizations and hand out awards for the gifts and talents of women. We can give ourselves credit for what we have already accomplished—and plan what we will do next.

*If I value myself and my accomplishments, the
validation of others will follow.*

Blame

"For wasn't she . . . somehow responsible for what was happening? Wasn't she in some way to blame?"

Paule Marshall, *Praisesong for the Widow*

"It's not my fault," we wailed as children, facing adults wrathful over broken vases, siblings in tears, and ink stains on party frocks. "I'm probably to blame," we mutter to ourselves now as we face our children's lies, our friends' betrayals, and our colleagues' manipulations.

Perhaps we blame ourselves because we'd rather ignore the faults of others and continue to live in a child's world of blind faith and optimism. We forget the difference between taking responsibility for our actions and shouldering blame that rightfully belongs to others. We need to see ourselves and others clearly, apportion blame fairly—and then do something about it. Blame itself is negative, sterile, and nonproductive because it only names; it accomplishes nothing.

I refuse to blame myself for the actions of others, and I accept the fault when it is mine and do something about it.

Flow

> *"When the Human Tribe allows the flow of life*
> *to set the rhythm, . . . harmony is found*
> *through subtle adjustments."*
>
> Jamie Sams, *The 13 Original Clan Mothers*

"Go with the flow." How idyllic the image: a stream of sparkling water sliding between soft green banks, moving steadily and evenly to the sea. Even an urban image of flow is pleasant: chains of cars sweeping safely and quickly to their destinations, no blinking red brake lights, no snarls. Peaceful flow.

In a crowd exiting a stadium we know it would be folly to try to move against the throng. Yet how often we deliberately set ourselves against the flow, internally and externally, refusing to adjust, setting ourselves in rigidity, snags in a stream snaring the debris of spring storms, nervous out-of-towners driving forty miles per hour on the interstate, making commuting miserable for everyone including ourselves.

When I go with the flow, obstacles melt before
me like frost in the sunshine.

August 29

Our Bodies

> *"Any woman who takes herself seriously must accept the responsibility of knowing and loving her body."*
>
> Marion Woodman,
> *The Owl Was a Baker's Daughter*

*S*ometimes we find it hard to accept our bodies because unnaturally thin, artificially beautiful women model the clothes we buy, sell the products we use, and entertain us. Because our bodies fall short of these idealized (and false) images of womanly beauty, we may reject them. We may even feel so disconnected from them that we don't recognize ourselves in mirrors. We prefer living in our heads because messy thoughts can be concealed; messy bodies can't.

Yet if we don't own and trust our bodies, we can't experience pleasure or express ourselves. When we block and repress our feelings, denying them expression, they stagnate and fester, sometimes causing physical illness. We need to claim our bodies with gratitude and nourish them with food, movement, and sufficient rest.

> *I will love the body heredity and nature have given me; it's the only container I have for my soul.*

242

Birthdays

"Because the birthday of my life
Is come. . . ."

Christina Rossetti, "A Birthday"

We honor our birthdays in different fashions, but it's important to mark them in some way rather than ignore them. Lives today often lack ceremony and ritual; certainly the day that gave us breath deserves commemoration.

Birthdays provide the opportunity to take stock—to look back on achievement and failure, happiness and sorrow, and to look forward with joyful anticipation. We can meditate on what we'd like to do differently in the coming year. We can spend the day in thanksgiving for the gifts we have received.

It's our day to do with as we like: isolate ourselves in solitude and reflection; try something new like a belly-dancing lesson, a nude swim, or a mountain hike; celebrate with friends; treat ourselves to an outfit, a massage, or a manicure; or honor the important people in our lives with gifts.

Although every day can be the birth of a new aspect of me, I will also honor my calendar birthday.

Management/Leadership

"Managers? All women are managers. That's
why they daren't give in to each other."
Dorothy Richardson, "The Ordeal"

*W*hether we manage households or
corporations, extended families or a
study group, we have a knack for managing others—along
with a suspicion of the concept of "management." We may
not like the idea of wielding power and control over others
nor the idea of handling the most minute details. We may
be more comfortable with management when we think of it
as leadership.

We can take the lead in managing resources and managing people because we have the experience. We've impro-
vised and stretched and "made do." We've talked a prissy
three-year-old into jeans instead of a party dress for a trip
to the livestock show, and we've stretched five pork chops
to feed seven. We know when to let others have their way
and when to supervise more closely. We know when model-
ing acceptable behavior and protocols is sufficient and when
more reinforcement is needed.

As a woman, I'm a natural manager—of
others and myself.

Challenge

*"One sank into the ancient sin of anomie
when challenges failed."*
Amanda Cross, *Death in a Tenured Position*

*C*hallenges keep us alive, interested, and interesting. They allow us to defy convention and expectations. They present us with opportunities to extend ourselves beyond what we may have thought it possible to do or be.

We relish challenges now because we're not afraid of risk, perhaps even because we think we don't have so much to lose. We challenge the status quo; if we, at fifty, want to return to careers in youth-oriented fields, why shouldn't we? We challenge authorities; if our doctor says we have to take estrogen because all menopausal women should, we'll do some research for ourselves before complying. We challenge familial and societal expectations. If we don't want to hostess the annual holiday dinner, we won't; if we want to marry a man ten years younger than us, we will.

*I accept the challenges life brings me — and
when life doesn't offer them, I'll challenge
myself.*

Little Lies

"And all these questions . . . cannot be dealt
with freely and openly by women; they must
charm, they must conciliate, they must—to
put it bluntly—tell lies if they are to succeed."
Virginia Woolf, *Professiors for Women*

*I*n midlife we give up what had become, for some of us, a habitual pattern of flattering, complimenting, cajoling, and "smoothing over" the truth. Trained from infancy to accept the necessity of social lies to gain approval and admiration, we also lied to conceal those parts of ourselves we feared were unacceptable and might bring us displeasure and disapproval.

We're willing to risk dislike now because we're more sure of ourselves. We also know that the daily practice of petty lying corrodes the brightness of our souls. We realize that if we cannot tell the truth, we cannot live our reality.

I will give up little lies and gain self-respect.

Distractions

"Don't be distracted."
Alice Munro, *Lives of Girls and Women*

ome of us thrive on distractions. We can be found standing at the kitchen counter, eating supper, talking on the telephone, and watching the TV while tightening a loose hinge on a cabinet door. But two hours later we may not remember what we ate, how the TV show ended, or whom we talked to, let alone why or what we said.

We could improve our concentration by eliminating distraction—taking the TV out of the study, the games off the computer, the books and newspapers off the dining table. We might even dare removing all projects but one from our desks. We could eat mindfully, exercise mindfully, and live mindfully. When we do, we may find we save time, for each action takes less time when we concentrate exclusively on it.

I will not allow myself to be distracted from the task of the moment.

Self-Esteem

> *"For healthy growth involves being able to give*
> *up our need for approval when the price of*
> *that approval is our true self."*
>
> Judith Viorst, *Necessary Losses*

Self-esteem is a gift of our age, for many believe women in our society can only be themselves before the age of twelve—and after the age of fifty. Self-esteem means believing in ourselves, defining ourselves in our terms, taking ourselves seriously, and insisting others do likewise.

We rejoice in our womanhood and our uniqueness. If we find ourselves in positions where we are nonessential, we leave those places and find others where we are needed. We do not numb our self-esteem or substitute other values such as service or nobility for it. We focus on current achievements, on what we have, not what we have lost. As we change and grow, we find new ground for self-esteem; as old friends and social activities lose their sparkle and interest, we find new ones.

> *There has never been, nor will there ever be,*
> *another woman just like me.*

Purpose

> *"Each day you let go by without exercising*
> *your will is a day lost to life."*
>
> Hallie Moore

We have to find and determine our purpose for living; otherwise, we feel useless. Without purpose, we resent our daily duties and obligations as a piecemeal giving away of ourselves. Our purpose doesn't have to be monumental—to make a million in the market, be elected to the state legislature, or write a bestseller—although it may be. We may simply determine to live purposefully every day—to care for ourselves, avoid hurting others, return what we receive, protect children, cherish the earth, be open to learn and willing to teach, love ourselves and others. So every day we accomplish something useful—make the doctor's appointment we've been putting off, write an overdue letter, call a friend, volunteer for story time at the library, weed a flower bed, read the article we clipped three weeks ago, cook a nutritious meal.

Purposeful living is productive.

September 6

Strength

> *"Women, he thought, when they are old enough*
> *to have done with the business of being*
> *women, and can let loose their strength, must*
> *be the most powerful creatures in the whole*
> *world."*
>
> Isak Dinesen, "The Monkey"

When we listen to women tell their stories, the strength it has taken to survive those lives amazes us. My writing group exchanged personal histories one afternoon. When we had finished, one said, "God, we're all tough broads." We laughed at the truth. Among us we had survived alcoholism and alcoholic parents, abuse, divorce, and the deaths of siblings and parents.

Sometimes we're inclined to dismiss our strength when we need to claim it. With strength we can battle the constant assaults on families, relationships, values, physical and emotional health, optimism, and spirituality. Our strength can be enough to turn this world upside down—when we realize, acknowledge, claim, and exercise it.

I am thankful for my strength.

Justice

"I was not going to argue about justice and
demand fair shares. That was beneath me. I
would manage on my own. Other women did."

Mairi MacInnes,
The New Yorker, 26 February/4 March 1996

W omen have received the short end of justice too often. When we first become aware of how unjustly we have been treated, we have a tendency to complain loud and long that "it isn't fair" or "it isn't right." And it isn't and hasn't been, and our complaints are valid. We should decide what we can do about it and then work for the cause of justice.

And sometimes we have to accept that life isn't fair, that we don't all share equally in all its riches. We must choose what we are going to do with what we have been given, even though others may have more wealth or more talents or an easier life.

Justice is a woman; I will remember that.
Maybe I'm the one who will remove her
blindfold.

Meddling

> *"She was in trouble with everybody in this house, and she deserved to be; as usual she had acted . . . meddlesome."*
>
> Anne Tyler, *Breathing Lessons*

Sometimes we just can't keep ourselves from interfering too much in the lives of others. We feel we know better (and maybe we do), but often the best thing we can do for others is leave them alone. We can't save our children from their mistakes any more than our parents could save us from ours.

Perhaps we meddle because we don't have enough outlets for our energy and our talents. We may be focusing on family and friends too much. If we find ourselves telling our daughters-in-law how to raise our grandchildren too often, we could teach parenting skills in a community outreach program. If we're constantly suggesting how our neighbors could remodel their houses, perhaps we could go build Habitats for Humanity.

What may be meddling in my home and family can be constructive and helpful in the larger community.

Time

"Delia wondered how humans could bear to live in a world where the passage of time held so much power."

Anne Tyler, *Ladder of Years*

When we feel time managing us, we can ignore clocks and simply do what we want, or have, to do without allotting arbitrary time limits to each activity. Time, after all, is not a dictator; it's a measurement. Our perception of time is subjective, but time itself is objective.

We could try living a day by our biorhythms—awakening naturally, eating when hungry, resting when tired, moving our bodies when energy needs to be released. What would that be like? If we're accustomed to being governed by time, we might find it frightening at first, but eventually liberating. Because autonomy is a benefit of being fifty, let's consider freeing ourselves from dependence on time. Let's wake up every morning knowing the day will be just long enough for whatever we have to accomplish.

Time is not the mistress of my life; I am.

Guilt

"We're guilty the minute we give birth."
Sally Ridgway

If we've done something wrong, then we need to admit it and make amends—the sooner, the better. But if we feel remorse or responsibility for something we haven't done, we need to let it go. Sometimes we make it too easy for others, especially our children, to induce guilt. We want to be perfect parents, but we're not. We want their world to be perfect, but it's made up of humans like us. So we blame ourselves for everything that does not work out as *they* would like. We say no to our adult children, who reply, "OK, Mom, but other mothers love babysitting their grandchildren for two weeks." We truly do love our grandchildren, so we feel guilty. We must free ourselves from this guilt. The world isn't perfect, and neither are we—and neither are our children.

No one can make me feel guilty if I refuse to accept it.

Mentors/Mentoring

*"Women are much less likely than men to find
authorities of either sex who are willing to act
as . . . mentors for them."*

Mary Field Belenky et al.,
Women's Ways of Knowing

ometimes we're so carried away with
our desire to achieve and succeed that
we ignore or trample younger women instead of bringing
them along with us. When we stand in splendid isolation
atop the peak, what does it gain our community if we
haven't left pitons in the glacier field so that others can
follow? When we break a glass ceiling, the powers-that-be
may quickly replace it unless we guard the entry hole. We
forget that private achievement is not as influential as
shared success.

Perhaps we fail to mentor more because we modestly
think we have nothing to offer. That assumption is wrong.
By providing models of successful women, we can change
the way both men and women view our sex.

*In sharing my experience and wisdom with
younger women, I perpetuate myself.*

Wisdom

> *"She touches the power of the feminine,*
> *a power which comes of* being, *not*
> doing . . . *the power of wisdom. . . ."*
>
> Judith Duerk, *Circle of Stones*

As we grow older, we increase in wisdom—practical, subjective intelligence, the ability to use knowledge acquired through study and living, an awareness of the manifold colorations and diversity of life. Through wisdom, we cope with uncertainty and the unexpected, grasp situations as a whole, and frame them in appropriate contexts. We teach others our wisdom while remaining open to continued learning ourselves.

The links between women, wisdom, and aging are ancient and strong. Throughout history, more goddesses than gods have been associated with wisdom: Sophia in Christian and Jewish tradition, Metis and her daughter Athena in Greek mythology, Isis in Egypt, and Tara in Tibetan Buddhism. Our culture often fails to venerate the wisdom of our elders. We can remedy that by respecting and listening to the wise-women we know and the wise-women we are.

I am woman; I am wise.

Nostalgia

"Nostalgia for him seizes her by the throat.
She fights against choking."

> Margaret Atwood, *The Robber Bride*

*N*ostalgia, the yearning for the way things used to be, is a bittersweet sentiment. Some of us, living in the present and anticipating the future, believe nostalgia best ignored or suppressed because we think nothing could be better than now. Others avoid thinking about the past because our personal pasts were sorrowful and tragic; we believe the past would best be left buried.

But we cannot prevent nostalgia. Sometimes it seizes us unawares as sensory impressions whisk us back to the past. Buttery biscuits breaking open from their own tenderness, fragrant steam rising, remind us of lazy Sunday breakfasts at the house of a favorite aunt. A flash of sun on the shores of a pine-encircled lake calls back summer camp when we were ten. A whiff of bay rum and a former boyfriend, startling blue eyes and crooked grin, returns.

Some things were better in the "good old days";
others were not.

Obsession

> *"There is a sort of instinct sometimes . . . to*
> *do things that seem to have no profit in them*
> *beyond the fact that they ought not to be*
> *done."*
>
> Geraldine Jewsbury, *Letters*

Sometimes we compulsively do that which we know will not serve us—we nag, we eat a second helping of "chocolate decadence," we make a spiteful comment. Fortunately we seem to be able to let go of obsessions now more easily than before. We don't so often obsess on weight, jobs, children, homes. We accept the five pounds we've gained, we find some value in the irritating coworker, we allow our son to be in college more years than we would like, we ignore dust collecting on the blades of the ceiling fan and under the beds. We know we aren't perfect—and neither is anyone else. Letting go of our compulsion for perfection, we can also abandon those actions that "ought not to be done."

Obsession is an enemy I can live without.

Truth-Telling

"The older woman becomes a 'truthteller.'"
Betty Friedan, *The Fountain of Age*

*M*idlife women tell the truth. We realize truth frightens as it fractures the complacent and the comfortable, but we also know it heals and restores. We are honest with ourselves and others because we know the value of truth. Self-aware, self-confident, and self-reliant, free from the expectations of external authorities, we tell the truth as we see it.

Truth, like a laser, removes blemished thoughts and words but must be wielded skillfully and carefully so as not to destroy the healthy tissue of our connections. When someone asks what we think, if we believe the truth will be hurtful, we can respond, "Tell me why you want to know." Then we can choose whether or not to answer. We distinguish between telling the truth for someone else's sake (usually unnecessary) and telling the truth for our own sake (usually necessary).

Speaking the truth with love and compassion, without judgment or sanctimony, seldom wounds.

Loneliness

> *"I was probably just going to have to go ahead
> and feel the aloneness for a while."*
>
> Anne Lamott, *Operating Instructions*

When we move jobs and residences, we know well the aching loneliness of the first days and weeks in our new homes. Sometimes there is nothing to do but embrace that loneliness and see what it has to teach us. Then as we begin to recover from the severing of our familiar roots, the shock of the transplant, we can move toward life in our new communities and end our isolation.

And sometimes we find ourselves alone when we did not choose it. We seem to be islands, surrounded by a sea of humanity, but with no apparent connection to anyone. What happens then depends on us. If we wish, we can extend ourselves to others and make the first gesture. Then we can attach ourselves to them and become a peninsula.

> *There are times in my life when I will be alone,
> and I never have to be lonely if I do not choose
> to be.*

Touch

> *"Physical touch is a concretization of the*
> *meeting of soul and spirit. Soul and spirit are*
> *given form in this way."*
>
> Jean Prétat, *Coming to Age*

*P*remature infants gain more weight and go home earlier if they are massaged daily. Bumper stickers ask, "Have you hugged your kid today?" When we give someone a brief backrub, we watch her tension melt away and her face soften. Touch connects mind and body, embodying our heart talk. Touch connects us with others when words fail. My friend Anne remembers meeting her high school English teacher shortly after she had given birth to a stillborn child. He knew of her loss just as she knew his wife had recently died. Wordlessly they moved into each other's arms for solace without speech.

Safe touching—a pat on the shoulder, a light touch of the hair, holding hands at the movies, hugging our good-byes—is one of the nicest gifts we offer one another.

I can express my emotions with touch as well as words.

Mercy

*"In the small events of daily living we are
given the grace to condition our responses to
frustration."*

Madeleine L'Engle, *The Irrational Season*

*E*xtending mercy to another person, perhaps even an undeserving person, is the gift of an expansive heart. When life overwhelms us with crushing burdens, and our spirits have been stretched beyond their natural elasticity, a gentle act of kindness, a smile from a stranger, the touch of someone's hand—an act of mercy—can bring us back home to ourselves again.

And when we in turn find ourselves thwarted, frustrated, and ready for revenge, we remember the mercy we have received. We catch the harsh words in our throats, quieten our voices, and forgive—"That's all right, I know it was an accident, I know you didn't mean it." We show mercy. And we are the better for it.

*In gratitude for the unmerited mercy I have
received, I will be merciful.*

Peace

"Whatever trials she had known she had transformed into tranquility."

Anzia Yezierska,
"Bread and Wine in the Wilderness"

              riday night, the end of a productive week, supper finished, dishes done, relaxing on the sofa with book or video, we know peace. There's nothing that must be done right now, nothing that can't wait. We find ourselves at peace with family, friends, and our sternest taskmasters, ourselves. And we've earned our peacefulness. The week was full of problems, letdowns, and disappointments through which we sturdily plodded. To have supper, we had to shop when we were tired. To be at ease with everyone, we have worked hard on our personal relations. And just now we feel ourselves complete, ready to quit doing and just be, no longer a puzzle in the process of completion, but finished, all the pieces in place, nothing left over.

I earn my peace; I will savor every moment of it.

Perception

*"Nothing that God ever made is the same
thing to more than one person."*
Zora Neale Hurston, *Dust Tracks on a Road*

s unique as the object observed—rose, dragonfly, poem—is the observer—you, me, Sally. No two of us will ever perceive anything in exactly the same way. If we ask five people what happened at the office today, we'll probably get five different responses. If we ask ten members of the audience to summarize our speech, no two answers will be alike.

So at this age we don't argue perceptions as much. If a friend hears someone's humor as clever while we find it sarcastic, so be it. We thought the movie romantic and touching while they thought it sentimental and cloying. So be it. Their judgment is no more clear or accurate than ours. They're just using different lenses.

*I will sharpen my own perceptions without
trying to make them agree with yours.*

Autumn

"It was a pleasant morning, mid-
September. . . . Such vigour came rolling in
from the fields and the down beyond. . . ."
Virginia Woolf, "The Death of the Moth"

*B*eing fifty reminds us of autumn, a season to harvest the crops of past achievements and plan future plantings. In Houston autumn is marked by "blue northers," brisk north winds that blow in, colliding headlong with Gulf Coast moisture, producing thunderstorms and heavy rains. But when the rains stop, the north winds prevail, humidity drops, and the skies turn an incredible pure blue, scoured clean of every wisp of cloud. The air sparkles like designer water, and Houstonians feel energized.

Just as we do at fifty. We've worked hard, and we have the harvest to show for it. Our storehouses overflow, but we're not resting. Winter hasn't yet arrived. We're busy skimming the seed catalogs for our next phase of living. Energy and excitement are hallmarks of autumn as well as ripeness and fulfillment.

In autumn I celebrate achievement, reap its
rewards — and plan my future work.

Safety

*"Safety and closure (and enclosure) . . . forbid
life to be experienced directly."*
Carolyn G. Heilbrun, *Writing a Woman's Life*

$\mathcal{W}$e want to be safe and secure, and we want to provide safety and security for those we love. But safety, especially when practiced as enclosure or confinement, stifles growth. Babies and toddlers confined to cribs and padded playpens may be protected from bumps and bruises at the cost of their self-development. None of us would choose to live life as bubble babies, handled only with rubber gloves, observed through Plexiglas—safe, but at the cost of human touch. Women protected by partners or society from unpleasant facts and harsh reality never grow—and should their protective environments be disturbed by a change in circumstances, illness, or death, run the risk of being destroyed.

*I know the difference between being protected
and being imprisoned.*

Competitiveness

"The way she sees it, it isn't personal:
whoever won't play doesn't like losing."
Louise Glück, "Cousins"

*C*ompetition originally meant "coming together" while a *rival* was someone with whom one shared a stream or waterway. When we think of competing as the act of coming together, then competitiveness becomes a positive quality. Comparing oneself with others to know where one stands can be helpful. Standing with others against a common foe often is necessary. Sharing the waterways of love, spirituality, and sisterhood would serve all of us.

Avoiding the winning/losing connotation of competition (and the occasional dirty tricks when winning becomes too important) while stressing sharing and community could help us deal with competition in all aspects of our lives.

I can be competitive when competitiveness
means equals coming together and sharing.

Style

*"Style allows the person to appear neither
inferior in one location nor superior in the
other."*

Maya Angelou,
Wouldn't Take Nothing for My Journey Now

We know that style has nothing to do with spring's hot new colors or fall's muted lipstick shades. Our style is the person we present to the world. We may be romantic, sporty, or tailored; what's important is that our style accurately reflect us. How we stand, act, move, and yes, how we dress and adorn ourselves, allows our essential selves to be revealed. No one can teach us style because style is individual; we are, after all, unique. If our style doesn't reflect us, if we try to dress and act as we are not, the incongruity jars, and we lose our balance and our sense of self.

*To have style is not the same thing as being
stylish. I reflect my style in everything I do —
as well as in how I dress.*

Rebirth

"*You will find yourself assisting at your own rebirth.*"

Maria Harris, *Jubilee Time*

At fifty we've lived a half-century; with luck we have a half-century to go. So why shouldn't we go through a rebirth to mark the occasion? The experiences of our first fifty years— growth, changes, transitions, loves, work, delights, sorrows—have been a crucible in which borrowed habits, thoughts, and feelings have been burned away, leaving our pure and true selves.

We know we have suffered losses, but we also know that rebirth of what has been lost is possible. Perhaps our skin loses some of its elasticity—and our spirit expands in balance, wisdom, and sense of humor. We lose strength and gain flexibility. We lose partners and friends and parents— and grandchildren are born and new relationships form, not replacements for what has been lost, but rebirths.

We can be reborn with each change, each passage, each transition.

Sovereignty

"Was ever people better ruled than hers?"
Anne Bradstreet, "In Honour of That High
and Mighty Princess Queen Elizabeth of
Happy Memory"

A question important in the early days
of the women's movement—and
perhaps equally important today—is whether women seek
to rule the world or just ourselves. Or both. In ruling ourselves well, we prove ourselves natural rulers. Since time
began women have been the keepers of ritual and wisdom
and responsible for the survival of the species. Perhaps now
is exactly the right time for us to assert our natural abilities not *over* but *with* men, to share the burden of ruling
when rulers are necessary.

At the minimum, we continue to exercise sovereignty
over ourselves, keeping a balance among all the women we
contain within, allowing our adult selves room to exercise
their talents while avoiding squelching our childish and adolescent selves. Then, if necessary, we can expand our sovereignty and rule others to their comfort and betterment.

*Of course women are fit to rule—and their rule
is fit.*

SEPTEMBER 27

Saying "No"

"What part of 'no' don't you understand?"
Martha Weathers

*M*artha Weathers, English department chair at my college, uses this sentence to terminate lengthy arguments from students insisting they be excused from course or college requirements. I've also heard this truth stated as "'No' is a complete sentence." Perhaps those of us who find it hard to say "no" need to post one of these sentences where we can see it every day. Answering in the negative may go against our nurturing instincts, our need to seek conciliation and consensus, our desire for emotional closeness. Yet ignoring our values and compromising our integrity by saying "yes" when we mean "no" weakens our effectiveness and our autonomy. Sometimes the only valid answer to a request is "no." We can take a deep breath, say it, and then walk away, reinforcing the message with our body language. We will find, perhaps to our surprise, that the world doesn't collapse.

I may not enjoy saying "no," but I can and I will.

Laughter

> *"Women laughed at themselves, they laughed at men, they broke up laughing and felt better, or, at any rate, less different—almost normal."*
>
> Jane Kramer, "The Invisible Woman,"
> *The New Yorker*, 26 February/4 March 1996

In midlife we find a new capacity to laugh as we acknowledge our role in the human comedy. Taking ourselves seriously also involves recognizing and admitting our foolishness.

My friend Martha has a wonderful laugh that starts deep in her guts with an audible rumble. The rumble intensifies as it rises, acquiring power from her diaphragm, finally exploding in distinctive, irresistible guffaws. Anyone would feel better after such a laugh. Laughter loosens the belly, making breathing easier, lowers the blood pressure, and relaxes the facial muscles. Laughter even aids healing as Norman Cousins points out in *Anatomy of an Illness*, the classic study of his recovery from an incurable illness with vitamin C . . . and laughter. Martha herself is a breast and lung cancer survivor, recovering with prayer, loving support . . . and laughter.

I will share a laugh with someone today.

Prayer

*"I know that prayer changes things. I know. I
don't question. I know."*

Maya Angelou, quoted in Sherry Ruth
Anderson and Patricia Hopkins,
The Feminine Face of God

*P*rayer can be formal, ceremonious, and structured or impromptu, simple, and quick—"please let the lump be benign," "may this 3 A.M. telephone call be good news," "thanks for friends." Prayer can be spoken, written, sung, danced, acted, painted, worked in clay. Work, acts of kindness, and self-expression can all be prayer.

We pray when we open our hearts and our souls and express what really matters to us—gratitude for the gifts of the day, regret for wrongs, petitions for tomorrow. We pray for help in our relationships with others and help in accepting ourselves, we ask for freedom for ourselves and others, we ask for open minds and good intentions, honesty and integrity. And while waiting for answers to our prayers, we go forward on our own.

When I want to pray, I am praying.

Living To Be One Hundred

"'I'll tell you a little secret. I'm starting to get optimistic.'"

> Bessie Delany in *Having Our Say:*
> *The Delany Sisters' First 100 Years*

It's certainly too early now to start planning our one-hundredth birthdays—or is it? The Census Bureau predicts there will be 1.2 million of us celebrating centennials in 2050. What will that be like? How will we look back from that birthday; what will we want our descendants and friends to say about us on that occasion? What do we want to have accomplished by then? How do we want to have lived?

Surely we will want to be acknowledged as positive, active, vital, future-oriented women who took responsibility for our own lives. Sometimes living in and through relationships, we were able to form new ones as we survived the deaths of family and friends.

On my one hundredth birthday, I want to be looking forward as often as I look backward.

Assurance

> *"There was about her an assurance, a*
> *carelessness, that he recognized as the*
> *signature of success."*
>
> Doris Lessing, "One off the Short List"

We've gained assurance as we've aged. Boldness, even audacity, underpins our self-confidence. We step forward with assurance and certainty into lives of value, usefulness, and purpose with the aid of helpful and trustworthy companions in a world of promise. We are full of assurance because we have proven ourselves to be capable women—capable of making decisions, managing our environments, planning our professional lives, and securing our financial goals.

And yet we're not careless with what we have. We've worked too hard to achieve our certainties to be casual about them. We've celebrated success with champagne, and we've drunk the gall of failure. We know life guarantees nothing unless we participate fully, exercising all of our talents.

> *Successful, self-confident, and assured—yes.*
> *Vain, arrogant, and careless—no.*

Belief

> *"They were so strong in their beliefs that there came a time when it hardly mattered what exactly those beliefs were; they all fused into a single stubbornness."*
>
> Louise Erdrich, *Love Medicine*

No longer do we cling to beliefs so narrow and rigid they paralyze us, so outmoded they no longer serve any useful purpose. No longer do we fear what will happen if we test our beliefs. On the contrary, we've learned that testing, then trusting, is the only valid path to belief. We test by reading, listening, and observing. Those beliefs that have weathered all of our experimentation, which have proven their truth over and over, form the foundation on which we build the rest of our lives. These mature beliefs liberate us from darkness; lift us to radiant, noble deeds; and enrich our spirituality.

Proven beliefs form the bedrock of my life.

Guilt

"A woman must prevail against her guilt and be willing to suffer it as the price she must pay for her freedom."

Judith Duerk, *Circle of Stones*

If we stay home with children, we're guilty of not sharing equally in the burden of paid work. If we work outside the home, we're guilty of causing domestic chaos. If we stay in touch with our adult children, we're interfering. If we don't invite them for Sunday dinner, we're unnatural mothers. If we spend a day in solitude, we're selfish. If we spend our time volunteering, we're busybodies who can't "let well enough alone."

We can't win. That's right. We can't. Accepting that we can't win is the first step in prevailing against our accusers—both internal and external. Because we can never be everything to everyone, let's drop the guilt.

If it's OK with you—and even if it isn't—I'm going to burn my membership card in Women of Guilt, Inc.

Storytelling

"Promise me, Soveida, that you'll listen to the stories women tell you. . . . Otherwise, how will you ever expect to understand the human heart?"

Denise Chávez, *Face of an Angel*

*W*hen my maternal grandmother was very old, she dictated her life story to her eldest daughter. Although outsiders probably would not find much of interest in this account of a schoolteacher and farmer's wife who raised four daughters and a son and survived the deaths of son, grandson, and husband, details such as her girlhood longing for a red dress instead of the blue ones her mother made to match her eyes are precious to me. Her pleasure over the births of her children and her comments on farming in Kansas form part of our family's *herstory*.

Midlife provides ample opportunity to consider telling, gathering, and recording our family stories, particularly the herstory of our women. In doing so, we too help our younger family members "understand the human heart."

I will record one of my stories today.

Fears of the Future

*"I have accepted fear as a part of life,
specifically the fear of change, the fear of the
unknown. . . ."*

Erica Jong, "Blood and Guts: The Tricky
Problem of Being a Woman Writer in the Late
20th Century"

We may be afraid because we don't know what's going to happen if we . . . change jobs, dump a partner, go back to school. Yet who does? Fears of the future may prevent us from change, and we know change is growth. We can let go of these fears because eventually they become pointless. Nothing bad has happened until it happens. What's coming may, in fact, be good, but if we worry too much now, we will be too emotionally exhausted to take pleasure then.

We should not belittle our fears of the future, but after utilizing them to remind us to take suitable precautions, we must plunge forward, refusing to let them prevent us from seizing life.

*The future sometimes terrifies me, but if I gaze
at it long enough, it becomes familiar and dear.*

Breathing

"Again, she breathed in. And what she took in was her own."

Carol Roh-Spaulding,
"Waiting for Mr. Kim"

*B*reathing is, from first inhalation to last exhalation, so much a function of life that we take it for granted unless illness or disease should make each breath a struggle. Then we acknowledge breath as the elixir of life indeed. In health it's possible—and desirable—to become conscious of breathing, too. To know how to use calm, slow breathing to relax tension and stress. To recognize that shallow breathing often indicates an attempt to defend against emotions and prevent their release. To be able to deepen our breath, let the energy flow, and recognize and deal with our emotions.

We honor breathing with the word *inspiration*, literally "inhaling air." But we've expanded that definition to include anything that stimulates our mind and emotions as much as oxygen, racing through the bloodstream, stimulates all our cells.

I breathe, I am alive.

Work

"Martha loved her work. She didn't have
to smile at it. She just did it. . . . Work,
honestly, was a piece of cake."

Fay Weldon, "Weekend"

When we love our work, it is "a piece of cake." Oddly enough, though, when we truly love our work, others may not regard it as work. Somehow today people expect that "real" work is something they grit their teeth to do, something they abandon in joyous relief Friday afternoon and pick up again Monday morning with despair and loathing. Where did they ever get such a negative view of work?

We know better. We know that meaningful work permits us to exercise our abilities and provides a field for our efforts. Important work keeps us alive and vital. Significant work is soul-making, not soul-destroying.

I care about my work, so I choose it carefully.

Emotions

*"Start thinking with your stomach. . . .
Emotions are born the moment you are
connected to something. . . . Become a
woman."*

Lynn V. Andrews, *Medicine Woman*

*W*hen we connect deeply with something or someone and feel that connection deep inside our gut, we cannot help becoming emotionally expressive. Some of us may avoid connection precisely because we fear emotion—why love what someday we may lose? Why open ourselves to friendship when friends sometimes betray? Why allow ourselves to feel compassion for one abused child when so many thousands demand our attention that we may be overwhelmed?

Yet when we permit ourselves to feel a full range of emotions, we find we do not have to be swept away by them. We can choose when to contain them and when to express them. Emotions do not have to be disowned or numbed; they can be integrated into our lives.

My life won't stop if I express an emotion.

Dreaming

> *"Dreams are the theater of the soul, our guide
> to the sacred."*
>
> Jean Benedict Raffa,
> *The Bridge to Wholeness*

*W*hen we begin living more consciously, we also seek more awareness of our unconscious life. We can access our unconscious through prayer, meditation, counseling, trance, visions—and dreams.

Sometimes our dreams seem primarily entertainment—a brief return to a happy childhood memory or a flight to a fantastic world where obstacles to happiness and creativity melt away. But when nightly we encounter threatening figures, appear in public naked, fail exams, or go on endless journeys, it seems clear a message is intended. Our unconscious tries hard to deepen our understanding of our own processes and the levels of our psyche we do not willingly visit in the daytime world. Dreams are another resource for conscious living.

> *Dreams can delight me, solve my problems, help
> me reach decisions, and show me a glimpse of
> the future.*

Cooking

> *"It is hard, and that's the truth of it, to have*
> *an easy-going nature over a hot stove."*
>
> Janet Burroway, *Opening Nights*

When our sons were teenage eating machines, I used to fantasize returning home with groceries, popping open the car trunk, walking into the house, and announcing, "Dinner's out there in the driveway, grab your forks and have at it." The infinity of cooking sometimes drove me to despair.

No wonder. We make a grocery list, drive to the supermarket, choose fresh, ripe, appetizing food, load it in a cart, check out, carry the groceries to the car, unload the car, make a delicious meal—sweet-and-sour soup, perhaps, with Chinese glass noodles in peanut sauce—and the food's devoured in ten or fifteen minutes, we clean up, and then, four or five hours later, everyone's hungry again.

> *I like to cook, but I'm not always good-natured*
> *about it.*

Adaptability

*"Human beings are special . . . which means
they can do anything."*

Leslie Marmon Silko,
"Humaweepi, the Warrior Priest"

daptability, thy name is woman.
Look at one of our days. A tearful
call before breakfast asks us to reconcile two quarreling
aunts. At work we present a proposal to the executive committee. Then we analyze funding for the project with the
accountant. During lunch with a daughter we discuss alter-
natives to day care. In the afternoon a secretary complains
of a tension headache, and we discuss how to alleviate
stress. Two competing health plans that we need to evaluate arrive in the mail. In the evening it's our turn to prepare dinner while we exchange news of our day with our
partner.

Woman—peacemaker, orator, financial planner, grandmother, healer, wisdom keeper, cook, decision maker,
confidante. Woman—fierce and tender, analytical and subjective, warrior and peacemaker. Yes, we are adaptable.

*I believe I can do almost anything I am called
on to do.*

Affirming Ourselves

> *"I need no warrant for being, and no word of sanction upon my being. I am the warrant and the sanction."*
>
> Ayn Rand, *Anthem*

*S*ometimes it seems all too easy to see mistakes and error everywhere, even (or perhaps especially) in ourselves. When we begin to criticize ourselves too harshly, we need to sit quietly for a time and think about what's right with us and what we like about ourselves. What about modesty and humility? Yes, what of them? Honestly recognizing and affirming our own worth is not the same as bragging about pseudo-accomplishments. What about recognizing and correcting our faults? Yes, we work hard at that as well.

We have many qualities to appreciate and cherish. Each day we say or do something to take pride in, and it's neither arrogant nor limiting to acknowledge that to ourselves.

One thing I really like about myself today is . . .

Reliability

"*She would be a base for members of the family. . . . She would be available, at everyone's disposal.*"

Doris Lessing, *The Summer Before the Dark*

We like to be thought of as reliable—dependable, trustworthy, honest, truthful, and responsible. But reliable as in dull, boring, bland, stiff, and monotonous? No, thank you. The first shows up for every board meeting on time; the second does, too—wearing the same suit and arguing the same point. Our worlds depend on most of us being reliable most of the time—and we are. But when we feel our reliability causes us to be taken for granted, we can cut loose and do something unlike ourselves, something thrillingly unexpected. Maybe a camping trip or a darkened backyard pool provides an opportunity to swim nude, something our stodgy selves would never consider—but we try it and we like it. Being true to ourselves sometimes means changing our minds—and our habits.

You can count on me. Just don't count on my always being the same person.

Dedication

> *"A woman who lives for a cause, a woman*
> *with dedication and unbreakable devotion—*
> *that's a woman who deserves the name of*
> *woman."*
>
> Kim Chernin, "The Proposal"

*D*edicated to political and social causes, dedicated to providing models for younger women, dedicated to eradicating ageism and sexism, dedicated to supporting our friends, families, spouses, and partners, we exemplify the noble quality of dedication. And in our dedication we can work miracles.

When we were younger, we were equally dedicated, but the objects of our devotion—social clubs, teachers, friends, entertainers, politicians—often proved unworthy. And when we discovered their flaws, sometimes we were crushed, thinking there must be something wrong with us. Today we know better. We're more discriminating about the causes and people to whom we give our devotion, but if they prove fallible, we know the fault is with them, not with our capacity for dedication.

I can be true without being blind.

Controlling Others

"There would be no powerful will bending hers in that blind persistence with which men and women believe they have a right to impose a private will upon a fellow-creature."

Kate Chopin, "The Story of an Hour"

*I*n midlife some of us awaken to the realization that our lives have gone along so smoothly because we have provided no resistance; we have let others bend us to their will. We have been compliant and obedient to their demands rather than the desires of our own hearts. Now we work toward self-realization and self-knowledge, making our sometimes painful way to autonomy.

Because of our experience, we know clearly that, with the exception of young children, we also have little right to impose our will on others. Even with children, we choose the areas in which to impose our desires and demands very carefully.

When I refuse to control others, I liberate myself as well as them.

The Ego

"Our egos are born delicate."
Mary Gordon, "The Parable of the Cave or:
In Praise of Watercolors"

The ego, the sense of self as distinguished from other persons and objects, is "delicate" at birth. It takes time for an infant to realize she and her mother no longer form the perfect union of the blissful nine months of gestation. But at fifty we've been through the terrors of separation and the despair of establishing autonomy. We know our egos can negotiate successfully between our passionate selves and our spiritual selves, judging when we can risk all for love or a cause and when to do so would be too injurious to ourselves and others. We've learned that our egos require acceptance, recognition, and achievement in just the right amounts. Too much and they may become too full of themselves, conceited, arrogant, overly ambitious. Too little and they become vengeful and jealous, belittling the accomplishments of others.

My ego, "born delicate," strengthened by experience, now functions as my lodestar.

OCTOBER 19

Concentration

"*My mind wanders—shameful! Remember:
CONCENTRATE. So are ALL things
done.*"

Mary Gray Hughes,
"The Thousand Springs"

*W*e affirm the value of daydreaming—and the value of concentra-
tion. Sometimes we put our minds in idle, letting them
drift over the smooth depths of the unconscious. And
sometimes we leap up, start the motor, and roar forward,
brimful of ideas we must work with *now* We know what a
waste it would be to let this urgency dribble away. So we
spring to desk or computer, pursuing those ideas until we've
run them to ground and committed them to paper or
screen—and only then realize we never ate breakfast, we
missed an appointment, we've got a crick in our neck, and
we're depleted. But the total concentration felt so good and
made us so aware of our strengths, perceptions, and sensi-
tivities that we can't be very sorry about missing anything
else.

Concentration makes me come alive.

Complaining

> *"But something is irritating me. The damn*
> *women haven't complained once, you*
> *understand. Not a peep, not a quaver, no*
> *personal manifestations whatever."*
>
> James Tiptree, Jr. [Alice Sheldon],
> "The Women Men Don't See"

*D*o women complain more than men? The male protagonist/speaker of this short story, along with two women and a pilot, has crash-landed in a swamp. He finds it astonishing that the women, far from complaining, accept the disaster with equanimity and sensibly set about making the best of the situation. Yet, isn't that what the majority of women have always done? When we think complaining will accomplish something, we can be loud and vociferous; when complaining will not help, we keep quiet. In either case, then we get on with doing something about the situation—working to oust the corrupt politician, raising the money to build a women's shelter, tutoring our less-educated sisters.

> *I complain when complaining will correct or*
> *improve a situation; when it won't, I keep silent.*

Simplifying Our Lives

"To say—is it necessary—when I am tempted
to add one more accumulation to my life,
when I am pulled toward one more centrifugal
activity."

Anne Morrow Lindbergh, *Gift from the Sea*

The question of what is necessary and essential for our happiness looms larger for us now as we reconsider and reevaluate our lives. How many telephones *do* we need? How many televisions? How many pairs of shoes? How many bathrooms and bedrooms for a household of two? If we eat 99 percent of our meals in the kitchen or breakfast room, do we need a formal dining room?

We also begin to question the necessity of many of our activities, those activities that pull us away from concentration, distract us from solitude, and absorb energy we would rather expend elsewhere.

I choose to focus my energy on my reasons for
living rather than my possessions.

Remembering the Past

*"The things we have tried to forget and put
behind us would stir again. . . ."*
Daphne du Maurier, *Rebecca*

Memories illuminate the present and help us understand why we sometimes, against reason, react positively to some people, situations, and places, and negatively to others. We need to recognize and acknowledge that we may not like a colleague because she sounds like the first-grade teacher who humiliated us by asking if we had wet our pants. Or that our sudden desire for a particular house may have less to do with its price and location than the towering tree in the side yard just like the one under which we played dolls.

Remembering the past, however, is not the same as living in the past. Living in the past means continuing to feel now as we did then, resenting, for example, siblings we felt were more loved than we. Remembering the past acknowledges that resentment and then releases it.

I recall my past to understand my present.

Busyness

> *"He had to admit she did keep busy. In fact,
> she was never still. She was as busy, he
> thought, as a canary in a cage, fluttering,
> picking, keeping up an incessant chirping."*
>
> Sally Benson, "Little Woman"

*P*erhaps life once required such busyness of us—more picking up, tedious chores, and repetitive, mind-numbing tasks than anyone should be expected to perform. So we quit. We learned that busyness is ultimately futile, something we—and our environments—could do without. Yes, we could shampoo our hair three times a day, dust daily, and mow our yards twice a week. We, too, like the look and feel of just-washed hair, reflections gleaming from polished wood, freshly mown yards as crisply edged as brush haircuts. But we know how fleeting those looks are, how much endless "fluttering" it takes to achieve them, and how boring it is to have no other accomplishments to chirp about at day's end.

*This canary left the birdcage of busyness
behind long ago.*

Attending Weddings

*"The implications of the wedding for the
spiritual welfare of humans are so profound
that within many religions it has attained the
status of a sacrament."*

Jean Benedict Raffa,
The Bridge to Wholeness

Attending weddings shows our support for their sacramental aspects. Our attendance represents our promise to form part of the communal support undergirding the tender structure of the new marriage. As we celebrate the joyful festivities with their families and friends, we bless the wedding couple. And in so doing, we bless ourselves. For those of us who are married, a wedding provides a splendid opportunity to renew our vows. As we thrill to the music and watch the bride and groom exchange rings and promises, our hearts remember our own weddings.

*An invitation to a wedding is an invitation to a
sacrament, and I will honor it as such.*

OCTOBER 23

Using Our Potential

> "She felt untapped, unused: as if she were
> the kernel of a walnut . . . withering in the
> shell. . . ."
>
> Fay Weldon, "And Then Turn Out the Light"

ow is exactly the right time to inventory our abilities. Are we using our potential, taking advantage of our talents, or are they lying dormant because we fear risk, criticism, or controversy? If we find ourselves wanting suddenly to crash through barriers, break tapes, and unleash something inside, then we feel the push of our potential. Perhaps circumstances have not yet permitted us to exercise our gifts in some areas— inside us, begging for release, may lie artists, dancers, managers, entrepreneurs, or spiritual leaders. We must permit ourselves to dream; what is it I've always wanted to try that I've never tried? Who do I feel stirring within, crying for a voice? Whatever form our potential takes, now is the time to release it. What have we to lose?

I'd rather be ripe and interesting than green or withered.

Passion

*"I grow more intense as I age. To my own
surprise I burst out with hot conviction. . . .
I want to put things right."*

Florida Scott-Maxwell,
The Measure of My Days

Sometimes we're surprised to find ourselves growing more passionate as we
age. We select the causes of our passion carefully—just
those that suit our talents, energies, and emotions. And we
stick with them; we don't switch rapidly from orphaned
chimpanzees to women's centers to homeless cats to Green-
peace to blood drives. We can afford passion now; we can
risk because we are emotionally, financially, and mentally
secure. We can rock our boats, letting ourselves be carried
away temporarily by our passions because we have compasses, rudders, and oars to bring us home to our stable
centers again. We will neither be swamped nor capsized by
passion.

*As a woman, I innately "want to put things
right"; I am comfortable with my passion for
causes.*

Movement

"Soon the girls were dancing without any audience, just dancing for the joy of movement, for the freedom. . . ."

Margarita Engle,
"Buenaventura and the Fifteen Sisters"

How good it feels to move—dancing, walking, swimming, skiing, bicycling, or whatever we choose. Our bodies were designed for physical activity; they respond to movement with joy and thanksgiving, rewarding us with a healthy glow, increased mental acuity, happier emotional spirits, even deeper spirituality. Movement is good for soul as well as body. Movement releases feelings, frees our spirits, and lets us know we're alive.

Dressing in soft, unrestrictive garments and easy shoes makes movement easier and more spontaneous. Wiggling toes, stretching arms, shaking out hands, curling over in a spinal roll, swinging our hips, moving our facial muscles, sashaying around the room—come on, let's shake it out right now!

Moving reminds me I am body as well as mind and spirit.

Gender Speak

"One of the most pusillanimous things we of the female sex have done throughout the centuries is to have allowed the male sex to assume that mankind is masculine."

Madeleine L'Engle, *The Irrational Season*

Some of us accept that male pronouns and male nouns such as *mankind* include everyone. Some would change gender-specific words to gender-neutral or gender-inclusive *mankind* to *humankind*. Some would change male nouns and pronouns to female ones to refer to both sexes—*mankind* to *womankind*. All of us are aware of how insidious using masculine words to explain the activities of all people can be, so we continue to sensitize ourselves and others. We question granting women "bachelor's" degrees, and calling Susan "Pete's widow" while seldom if ever referring to Pete as "Susan's widower." We ask if those who distrust women are called misogynists, and those who distrust people in general are "misanthropes," why is there no word for those who distrust men?

I will be sensitive to the gender implications of the words I use to refer to myself and others.

Excellence

"She had known what it was to take excellence for granted. That was the difference between them."

Mavis Gallant, "His Mother"

*W*e, too, have known what it is to take excellence for granted because we've lived long enough to experience it in many forms—at work certainly but achievement in other areas as well. We've known those who exemplify excellence in their endeavors—spiritual leaders such as Mother Teresa, artists such as Georgia O'Keeffe, writers such as Annie Dillard, musicians such as Joan Baez, dramatic performers such as Katharine Hepburn, gardeners such as Tasha Tudor, mothers and friends such as our own. Yes, we know the difference between excellence and mediocrity.

Yet, do we really take excellence for granted simply because we're familiar with it? I doubt it. Given human fallibility, excellence is simply too rare. But that doesn't mean we cannot strive for it, and recognize, approve, and applaud it where we find it.

Striving for excellence is a worthwhile goal as long as I am reasonable about it.

301

Self-Pity

*"I don't see why my pleasure with self-pity
should give anyone else a bad opinion of me
or why I should care."*

Alison Roe, "How I Became a Single Woman"

*M*ost of us succumb at times to self-pity and why not? Surely we all have reason to feel at times very sorry for ourselves. What's wrong with indulging in some tears when we seem unfairly singled out for injustice and pain?

Perhaps we believe self-pity to be a particularly female frailty; however, Aristotle speculated that all pity is basically self-pity. So when we allow ourselves to feel sorry for ourselves, we soften and open our hearts to the sorrows of others. And, as Alison Roe points out later in this essay, when self-pity recedes, or when we want to emerge from our morass of despair, we decide what we can do about our misery—and we usually plunge into productive activity.

*I don't mind indulging in self-pity when the
occasion warrants; I won't stay there forever.*

Sleep

*"All I really loved to do was sleep. . . . Nine,
ten hours, and I'd wake up on my belly, lift
my arm off the pillow and it would drag a
sleeve of dream. . . ."*

Mona Simpson, "Victory Mills"

Sleep researchers say we're sleep-deprived if we need an alarm to wake us; sleep is probably the area we neglect most frequently in taking care of ourselves. We simply don't get the sleep our bodies require, either because we aren't in bed long enough or because of the insomnia that frequently accompanies menopause and stress.

What can we do to gain nature's restorative powers? If naps work for us, we can take them unashamed. Going to bed earlier, asking people not to call after 9 P.M., avoiding evening stress, reading, listening to music, bathing, and drinking herbal tea can be helpful. When insomnia strikes, we can reassure ourselves that lying in bed, emptying our minds, relaxing our muscles, and keeping our eyes closed is also restful.

I will take advantage of the blessing of sleep.

Indulgence

*"There is a mistaken idea . . . that an
overdose of anything from fornication to hot
chocolate will teach restraint by the very
results of its abuse."*

M. F. K. Fisher,
"Once a Tramp, Always . . ."

$\mathcal{B}$y midlife we've probably got a grip
on indulgence, walking happily and
moderately between excessive indulgence with its possibilities of physical illness, addiction, and financial problems,
and puritanical self-control that denies all pleasures. We've
discovered ways to gratify appetite without undue harm.
We indulge an appetite for fashion by shopping thrift stores,
buying scarves instead of dresses and luxurious hose rather
than cashmere sweaters. If we absolutely adore strawberry
shortcake, then when strawberries are in season we make a
meal of an absolutely perfect one with everything we long
for—freshly baked butter biscuit, sliced berries sweetened
with sugar, home-whipped cream. Appetite indulged, we
can easily forgo eating any others that are less than perfect.

An occasional spree does me no harm.

Powerlessness

> *"Women often feel powerless to initiate change, whether in their personal lives or in the public sphere."*
>
> Harriet Goldhor Lerner,
> *The Dance of Intimacy*

We recognize the two sides of powerlessness, one constructive, one destructive. All of us, men and women, are powerless over some of life's circumstances. We cannot control AIDS, cancer, or the drunk driver in the next lane. We accept our powerlessness in these areas and trust our personal higher power. Submitting to this existential powerlessness is paradoxically empowering; as we accept our humanity, letting go of what we cannot control, we claim power for doing what is humanly possible.

But we cannot and should not accept powerlessness based on inequality and victimization. Women do not have as much power in our society as we should have. We need power because power gives us the freedom to be who we are and do what we want. We fight this powerlessness as we should.

To be powerful means to accept some areas of powerlessness.

Self-Hatred

> *"Isn't it time for women to break those chains*
> *of oppression? Isn't it time for that endless*
> *cycle of self-hatred to cease?"*
>
> Denise Chávez, *Face of an Angel*

Sometimes no one can be harder on us than us. We flagellate ourselves for the most minor of faults, sometimes attacking ourselves, not just for our deeds and misdeeds but attacking our egos themselves.

Perhaps it helps to understand that such extreme self-hatred is actually the worst form of arrogance and pride. If we didn't expect perfection of ourselves, we'd hardly be so critical. And yet, we also need to give up a short-sighted view of our talents that makes us settle for less than we are—and hate ourselves for doing so. We need to give up perfection, accept fallibility, and love ourselves, stifling the voices of self-hatred the minute they start their insidious whine.

I don't really have time to hate myself anymore.

Independence

"'The time may come—in fact does come to everyone—when we have to decide something important on our own, be responsible perhaps not only for our own lives and fortunes, but those of other people.'"

Vera Brittain, *Testament of Youth*

We're glad we're independent in those moments when we have to act alone, when not only our own happiness may rest on our abilities, but also the destinies of others. Whatever it takes to strengthen independence, we do, so that when we must act independently on a moment's notice, we can. We practice independence—living temporarily in a city where we know no one, managing household finances, hiring and supervising workmen.

Then when the service provider tries to cheat us, when we lose our way in a strange city, when the rising water catches our car halfway across the bridge, we are ready.

Having people to depend on is wonderful; so is knowing I am one of those people.

Place

*"Wondered which had changed the most, place
or self? It was a strong place."*

E. Annie Proulx, *The Shipping News*

Strong places stand out in our memory.
Some of mine are London streets and
parks, Haystack Mountain in Vermont, Glastonbury Tor,
the red rock hills of Sedona, Arizona, and the rugged coast
of Big Sur. We feel drawn to these places, and we honor
them for their spiritual attraction even when we cannot
explain that pull to anyone else.

When people hear me rhapsodizing about a place in
Texas, they ask, "Is it on the water?"

"No."

"Well, then it's on a golf course?"

"No."

"So the scenery must be magnificent?"

"Not exactly—limestone, mesquite, cactus, cedar, and
oaks." They walk away puzzled. I can't explain the attraction I feel. It's simply one of my "strong places." I'm glad
I have them. I hope all of us do.

*Some places attract me spiritually; I will find
my way to them as surely as the monarch
butterflies return to Mexico.*

Giving and Receiving

*"How can I give it, Clara, how can I give it if
I don't have?"*

Tillie Olsen, "Tell Me a Riddle"

*G*iving and receiving center our lives as
women. Yet we know, as Tillie Olsen's
protagonist says, that we cannot give what we have not
received. Her protagonist speaks of material poverty, but we
know spiritual and emotional poverty as well. Yes, we give
gladly, but when the basket is empty, we take whatever measures are necessary to replenish our stores. We do not
always have to teach; sometimes we need to be taught. We
do not always have to direct our attention outward; sometimes we must pay attention to our inner existence. We're
so much wiser about receiving now; we know it's neither
indulgent nor selfish to take what is offered. We know now
that we give to others when we permit ourselves to receive
what they offer.

*I love to give, and I am learning to receive with
an equally full heart.*

Goddess

> *"The reemergence of the Goddess in*
> *contemporary culture . . . is a new naming of*
> *women's power, women's bodies, women's*
> *feelings of connection to nature, and women's*
> *bonds with each other."*
>
> Carol P. Christ, *Diving Deep and Surfacing*

*F*or those of us who reject an exclusively male God, the Goddess has enormous appeal. First of all gods was She, the earth goddess whose beautifully female images date from 7000 B.C. Her fertility, abundance, and connection to Mother Earth stir ancient chords within us. In Her, we see ourselves as fully alive, fully female, nurturing and comforting *and* powerful.

For the Goddess, as Astarte, Inanna, Ishtar, and Nut, was also "Queen of the Heavens," worshiped as lawgiver *and* lifegiver, valiant leader *and* eternal mother. Becoming aware of Her worship as practiced in earlier cultures reveals the clear truth of divinity, free of the fog of patriarchal bias.

> *Made in the image of both God and Goddess, I*
> *will worship the Goddess within me.*

Harmony

"*Harmony happens when behavior and belief come together. . . .*"

Jean Shinoda Bolen, *Gods in Everyman*

*H*armony becomes an attribute of midlife, the welcome result of abandoning masks and pretenses to "walk our talk." How serene we are when we are in harmony with ourselves and the universe. How good it feels to appreciate all our aspects from glorious to inconsequential, neither inflating our positive qualities nor focusing on our flaws.

When we feel ourselves clanging rather than chiming, we recognize disharmony. We note the jarring effect on our psyches of being out of step and out of sync, unhappy with ourselves and everything and everybody. We understand that circumstances have made us do something against ourselves, so we correct that misdeed. Then, like the glass harmonica, which produces a hauntingly lovely melody when stroked, we too become melodious with peace.

When I am in harmony with myself, I live in harmony with others.

Learning

*"She'd discovered learning was like the window
over her bed, a place to see out."*

Maureen Brady, "Corsage"

When we stop learning, we stop living. In the current information age, we worry more about overload than about ignorance, but being bombarded with information is not learning. We learn when we make information our own, filtering it through our sensibilities and making a place for it in our world order.

Learning is not necessarily academic. Learning is being curious, checking an atlas when the evening news mentions an unfamiliar geographical area. Learning is tracking down the lyrics to a song your children or grandchildren like. Learning is memorizing a favorite poem while you iron or make soup. Learning about the latest computer software, a social program, or bestsellers, and learning where to go for information, keeps us young and vital.

*Learning is a lifelong task; I make my life
longer by learning.*

Faults

> *"I know my faults so well that I pay them*
> *small heed. They are stronger than I am.*
> *They are me."*
>
> Florida Scott-Maxwell,
> *The Measure of My Days*

lthough we're accustomed to trying to eradicate our faults, at midlife we begin to accept some faults as part of our common share in human fallibility. Perhaps some are ultimately ineradicable, such as the only physical imperfection of the beautiful woman in the Hawthorne story "The Birthmark." When her husband attempts to perfect her by removing it, she dies, for it was an inextricable part of her human nature.

We face our faults and acknowledge them because we know awareness is the key to working with them. When we realize we become patronizing when explaining something more than twice, we watch for that tendency when working with tyros. When we know our conversational "hot buttons," we'll observe our reaction to those topics before plunging into an argument.

> *I'm human, I'm flawed. My faults are part of*
> *my humanity.*

Being Sensible

> *"You see, I'm one of those people who live*
> *sensibly and sanely. . . . I've had my*
> *moments, and if I had it to do over again,*
> *I'd have more of them."*
>
> Nadine Stair,
> "If I Had My Life to Live Over"

*W*hen someone proposes a midnight bike tour, Sensible replies, "Oh, I couldn't possibly give up my eight hours of sleep." And gives up instead the once in a year—or lifetime—experience of sweeping through eerily deserted city streets, silent except for the swishing of hundreds of bike tires, watched by coldly remote stars, brushed by night air, fueled by an adrenaline rush. Yes, it would be more sensible to stay in bed, but. . . .

Of course we choose to live sensibly most of the time—we take care of our bodies—but we're open to moments. When our hearts leap in response to a summons or an invitation, we say yes, by all means.

Life is more than being sensible; life is also
risk and adventure.

Presents

> *"My husband gave me a broom on Christmas.*
> *This wasn't right. Nobody can tell me it was*
> *meant kindly."*
>
> Grace Paley, "An Interest in Life"

omen generally choose gifts so carefully that a present this thoughtless would break our heart. What makes a present special is the depth and richness of the associations it evokes between giver and recipient. We attended a marvelous sixtieth birthday party the past summer. The honoree's wife had flown their children and their spouses in as a surprise—a wonderful gift of *presence* as present—and the children gave their dad a video of his life that they had produced. Another friend gave her husband several rounds of golf at outstanding courses—an especially nice gift for she doesn't play and wouldn't be accompanying him. A writer friend was moved to tears by her husband's gift of a beautiful leather journal inscribed with her name.

The best presents demonstrate how well the giver
understands the recipient.

Evil

"It can be argued that evil is not the reversal
of good, but the vacuum of good."

Estela Portillo Trambley, "The Burning"

*E*vil flourishes when ignored. Evil chuckles when our response to the death of children in Israel is being glad we don't live there. Evil smiles when we hear of fourteen-year-olds committing robbery, and we call the security company to upgrade our alarm system. Evil grins when we fail to correct a malicious rumor. When we ignore the opportunity to do good, we permit evil.

Someone stumbled and I didn't reach out a hand. Someone cried with hunger while I finished my supper. Someone went to prison and I voted to build more. Someone lived on the street and I detoured around her. Someone approached my car to sell me a flower and I locked the door.

*Every good deed, every kind word, every soft
touch forms a barrier against evil.*

Rigidity

"There we stop; there we stand. Rigid, the
skeleton of habit alone upholds the human
frame. Where there is nothing."

Virginia Woolf, *Mrs. Dalloway*

How often we used to stand frozen,
unable or unwilling to bend, give in,
accept, or thaw. How painful to be separated from what we
yearned for by the ice of rigidity, custom, or fear. We no
longer cling to habit and familiarity, we no longer fear the
unknown, the flush of spring torrent unclogging the detri-
tus of our lives, or the juiciness of sap rising in our veins.
We no longer fear bursting into laughter or tears or anger
because such is the nature of living beings. In rigidity, there
was *no-thing*. No thing new, no thing different, no thing living. Just us, as rigid as masts, dead trees, unable to weather
wind and storm as living trees do.

*I thank the Creator for helping me relax my
rigidity.*

Needs and Wants

"'I don't know,' she said; 'sometimes you can want something a whole lot, only to find out later that it wasn't what you needed *at all.'"*
Alice Walker,
"A Sudden Trip Home in the Spring"

Once we've satisfied our basic human needs for food, shelter, companionship, security, health, love, and work, what else do we really need? Desire so easily slips on the mask of necessity, whispering slyly in our ears that we really, truly *need* that . . . heavy gold bracelet, third telephone, luxury sedan, towering orchid plant. How can we throttle desires while honoring the quiet needs our soul requires?

One way to differentiate between needs and desires is to ask ourselves what difference acquiring something or satisfying a want will make in our lives tomorrow, next month, or next year. We can also refuse to compare our needs and desires with those of others—our necessities are as unique as we are.

Sometimes I need what I want, sometimes I don't, but I'm learning the difference.

Focus

"She sits at the kitchen table, concentrating on her outlines. . . ."

Bobbie Ann Mason, "Shiloh"

Sometimes now we find ourselves able to return to the blissful state of childhood when our ability to focus on one activity to the exclusion of all others, even things we normally liked, was unparalleled. We could not be distracted and had sometimes to be forcibly pulled away from the object of our concentration. What pleasure that concentration brought then! How we welcome the return of focus now!

When we find ourselves trying to focus on too broad a range of interests, when we spread ourselves too thin over the bread of daily life, we can limit or narrow our activities. We can remind ourselves that when we focus, we get more accomplished. We understand that interrupted tasks end up taking two or three times as long to finish as those on which we work uninterrupted.

I honor activities, objects, and people when I focus on them.

Imagination

> *"My awe is not for the silence and space of the endless universe but for the inspired imagination of man [sic]. . . . "*
>
> Katherine Anne Porter,
> "The Future Is Now"

Imagination enriches every age and stage of our lives. With imagination we can travel anywhere, fantasize our future, and embellish our actual experience. Imagination compensates for poverty of place or situation, replacing the actual with the desired. Imagination combined with experience stocks the palaces of our minds with glittering, golden inventories. Imagination redeems the past, enhances the present, and helps us envision the future: "What would it be like if I . . . ?" Those fantasies, those "imaginings," then can become our reality.

How do we supply the imagination? Reading, listening, observing, and dreaming—and allowing ourselves sufficient time to exercise those faculties.

With imagination I need never be poor or lonely or afraid.

Speaking Out

*"My business in life has been to think and
learn, and to speak out with absolute freedom
what I have thought and learned."*

Harriet Martineau, *Autobiography I*

Speaking out is something most of us
have gotten very good at over the years.
We've learned, sometimes painfully, that if we don't speak
up to defend ourselves, many times no one else will either.
We've also learned that it is our duty, privilege, and responsibility to speak up for those who cannot—infants and children, women battered into silence, those defeated by illness,
the elderly, those whose education has not permitted them
the language to speak for themselves.

We've learned to do our research, to investigate our
hearts and consciences, and then, when we are sure we are
right, not to whine, not to nag, but to speak up, arguing
logically and calmly and passionately when necessary.

I want my way and I shall have it.

Religion

*"At once go and make them change. Tell them
to write: Race, human: Religion, none."*
Tillie Olsen, "Tell Me a Riddle"

*T*he cynicism reflected in this quotation does not mirror the religious
feelings of most of us. Polls show that the majority of the
baby-boomer generation believe in life after death and
consider themselves religious. Yet it is true that many of
us have abandoned the denominations of our youth, and
some, tired of interfaith bickering and divisiveness, are religious without belonging to synagogue or church, mosque or
fellowship.

Midlife seems to be a good time to search for meaning,
to reconsider the value of material prosperity, and to submit to discipline—all aspects of religious faith. To be religious is to accept the existence of a higher power, to accept
that we are not the be-all and end-all of existence. We find
that comforting.

*Religion helps me face the terrors of the day
and the night.*

Inspiration

"Inspiration is that voice in my head that
keeps talking."

Hilma Wolitzer, "Twenty Questions"

Sometimes we absolutely think we can't do it anymore—the project's impossible, the relationship foundering, our skills inadequate, our coworkers incompetent. Yet when we quit caterwauling, we hear the quiet voice of inspiration saying "I think I can." Once at a poetry reading, a woman walked up to read with tubes trailing from her nostrils down to the oxygen canister she carried on her back. Smiling at her husband, she commented, "I brought my 'inspiration' with me today." And so she had—she had brought the literal life-giving stuff, the breath she required, and she had brought her emotional and spiritual inspiration, her husband. She also provided inspiration by life, example, and work for the rest of us who, for a few hours at least, gave up complaining about the domestic and professional obstacles we thought prevented us from writing.

I remember that inspiration comes from
without—and within.

NOVEMBER 19

Respect

*"What bound them was the democracy of
respect for each other's work, a confidence in
themselves and in each other."*

Doris Lessing, "One off the Short List"

What binds us one to another is often respect. Sometimes it's respect for work, but it's also respect for values, for lives lived, discipline demonstrated, and compassion exemplified. Mutual respect. How good it is to work and play with people we respect. How nice to stand shoulder to shoulder with our sisters and brothers, a democracy of equals, no one elevated above others to be awarded a gold medal. This is camaraderie of the highest order, the best of the best. We will work to guarantee that we always deserve respect.

*I will remember that respect is hard to earn
and easy to lose.*

Justice

> *"Life was unjust at the best of times and was only denying me briefly what it denied other women for a lifetime."*
>
> Mairi MacInnes,
> *The New Yorker*, 26 February/4 March 1996

*M*ost women become acquainted with injustice at some point during our lives—penalized for our sex when sex should not have been a consideration, perhaps denied opportunities or bonuses or job security. Familiarity with injustice, however, does not breed indifference. Some of us become militant in midlife, when something finally punctures our immunity from injustice, and we realize at last what other women have been suffering all along. So we march, picket, and protest. We work to elect and appoint judges who treat women equally and fairly. We join political-action committees and organizations. We work with the victims of injustice, becoming child advocates or helping with women's shelters. And we run for political office so that we can work within the system for change.

Working for justice is a powerful midlife freedom.

Loyalty

> *"I think women tend to be loyal. I just think*
> *we work differently; I think we're more task*
> *oriented, more cooperative."*
>
> Maggie Williams, quoted in
> Henry Louis Gates, Jr.,
> *The New Yorker*, 26 February/4 March 1996

Women are innately cooperative, sharing, and loyal. When we were younger, our loyalties may have been misguided. But we're sophisticated enough now to realize that many of those who once had our loyalty no longer (and perhaps never did) deserve it. Because we're wise, with powers of discrimination whetted and honed on the sharpening stone of experience, we no longer go to battle for clay statues. People full of bull do not deserve—or receive—our loyalty. Discarding the unworthy leaves us more energy for loyalty to those who earn it. At our age, our loyalties run deeper and fewer.

I cannot be loyal to a faulty cause or person.

Procrastination

> *"Procrastination is pushing aside or putting off. . . . It is thinking the moment is tomorrow. It is a way not to let in vital energy."*
>
> Natalie Goldberg, *Wild Mind*

I procrastinate. Even though I knew where to find this quotation, first I reread some favorite passages in Goldberg's book—thirty minutes. Then I glanced at the dog and realized he needed a brushing—fifteen minutes. I browsed through my CDs— ten minutes. Then I remembered I hadn't selected poetry for a reading next week—ninety minutes. And then it was bedtime with no meditation written.

A cure for procrastination that works—when I remember to use it—is making deals with myself. I should have told myself I could reread Goldberg's book—after I had written for fifteen minutes. Once I get started with something I like doing, then I usually lose myself in it. Chances are I would have written five or six meditations before I remembered my promised reading.

Procrastination reminds me to pay attention to what I'm doing.

Struggle

*"Now I've come to believe that there is no
central act; instead there is a central struggle,
ongoing. . . ."*

Janet Sternburg,
"The Writer Herself: an Introduction"

While we wait for the defining act that will change the course of our lives, we make the small decisions that determine our life paths in the struggles of every day. To enter a different profession after retirement, we cannot simply move into it on a certain calendar day. For months and even years before that day, we prepare ourselves, researching, taking classes, even changing geographical location if necessary—an ongoing struggle to define ourselves in terms of what we want to do.

Certainly sometimes it seems as if we have acted impulsively—leaving a relationship or quitting therapy or moving. But if we examine those actions later, we will find we had been grappling with the decisions, consciously or unconsciously, for months before.

*I must struggle every day to continue to define
myself in my own terms.*

Promises

> "It might have been coincidence. It might have
> been how she kept her promise."
>
> Barbara Wilson, "Miss Venezuela"

Whether we keep our promises with lighthearted joy, grudging obligation, or somewhere in between, we keep them. Recipients of broken promises too often in the past, we believe in the promise of promises. So we honor them faithfully. However, we're also more careful about making promises. We don't accept unconditional promises—promise me you won't laugh, promise you won't get angry, promise you'll do this one little thing for me. These promises don't work, and we're too smart to agree to them. Nor do we demand them of others. We won't be like Nebuchadnezzar, asking his court magicians not only to interpret his dreams but also to recount them, for it seems he had forgotten them.

It's easier to keep my promises when I'm careful about the promises I make.

Gratitude

> *"The purest and noblest love of the olden time is*
> *that which draws from its annals motives of*
> *gratitude and thanksgiving for the past. . . ."*
>
> Frances Manwaring Caulkins,
> *History of New London, Connecticut*

This is a good season of the year and of our lives to remember the blessings we too often take for granted. So let's be grateful for:

partners who love, protect, and empower us,

friends who share tragedies and triumphs,

children who model creativity and consciousness,

those whose daily work makes our lives safer, easier,
    and more comfortable,

the arts and artists,

the blessings of nature—cedars, peacocks, rainbows,
    spider lilies, and chipmunks,

technology—potable water, air conditioning, central
    heat, telephones, and computers,

health and the resources and medicine to maintain it,

and being born women.

> *As the yogis say, I will practice an attitude of*
> *gratitude today and every day.*

November 26

Role-Playing

*"Born and reborn to a splendid image, she had
never looked for her self, nor had anyone else."*
Rona Jaffe, "Rima the Bird Girl"

$\mathcal{W}$e assume many roles in our lives—
perhaps as many as we have changes
in our wardrobes. We may have been Cub Scout den mothers, cheerleaders, waitresses, single moms, corporate wives,
lawyers, lovers, freedom fighters. Once I mothered three
children, the oldest of whom had just turned four, played
competitive tennis, worked with ceramics, and experi-
mented with gourmet cooking. I don't do any of those
things anymore—those roles no longer fit.

To remain authentic, periodically we check the fit and
appearance of the roles we accept and alter or discard those
that no longer suit us. We let our real selves dominate the
parts we play rather than letting the roles become our real
selves.

*I will examine my roles as carefully as I
examine my wardrobe and throw out the ones
that no longer reflect the real me.*

Quarreling

"Do I intentionally bend my tone
to intentionally provoke you. . . ?"
Hallie Moore, "Breakfast Table Small Talk"

*Q*uarreling can be healthy and productive or poisonous and destructive. It's healthy to stand up and defend ourselves. It's healthy to quarrel when something can be corrected, when someone needs to be told he is wrong. Quarreling is healthier than stewing in silent resentment. But bickering day in and day out over trivialities is destructive. Maybe we don't realize a thousand tiny cuts can kill a relationship just as easily as one gigantic slash.

Although it's often good to walk away from a fight, sometimes standing toe to toe for ten minutes or so and screaming, yelling, and ventilating is just what's needed. Then we separate and cool off, and later, when we're calmer, we can sit down and peaceably analyze our disagreement.

I will choose my quarrels carefully and not
waste my energy in useless bickering.

Adventure

"You know, if you stay stifled where you are,
you're dead before you're dead."

Eda LeShan, quoted in Fhillip Berman and
Connie Goldman, Eds., *The Ageless Spirit*

When we lead adventurous lives, we wake up each day full of wonder about what's going to happen next. Taking risks, we find ourselves more alive at this age than ever before. We do things we never thought we'd do—ride the highest roller coaster in the world, swim with the whales, take a month's holiday alone. We surprise ourselves and that's terrific.

We show our younger sisters what aging means—the freedom to dare, to take journeys rather than wait, to be flexible rather than stiff. Our adventures can be inward as well as outward. We can change our philosophies, learn other disciplines, study new fields, and make passions of subjects we once had time only to make interests.

Midlife is full of adventure, and I'm going to get me some.

Family

"But why couldn't she do what she longed to do? Why, with all her passionate sympathy for them, should any actual contact with her people seem so impossible?"

Anzia Yezierska, "Children of Loneliness"

We love our families, yes, we adore them—and we wish we never had to spend another minute with them. No one can exhilarate and infuriate us more than family. No one can stifle or empower us more than family. No one can smother us and abandon us more than family. We do our best to live with the seething caldron of emotions families engender. Most of us separated physically from our birth families long ago, and many of us have psychically separated as well, having reached a point where we can regard them with compassion and objectivity.

In the families we have created, we've established boundaries that permit us individuality within the family group so that we can have both solitude and companionship.

Living in family provides an antidote for loneliness—and protection for solitude.

Leisure

"Leisure, a genuine respite at the end of labor, became what it largely remains today, a masculine prerogative."

Rosalind Miles,
The Women's History of the World

We don't believe life should be oriented to leisure, but we also know we require leisure to replenish ourselves. Leisure doesn't mean seven or eight hours of sleep. Leisure is relaxing and looking at photo albums, sitting comfortably and listening to a favorite tape all the way through, lingering over dinner with friends, taking a few hours for a beauty treatment. When we find leisure being omitted from our daily routines, then we must restore its place. When both husband and wife work, where is it written that he may sit down with the paper after they get home while she goes to the kitchen to start dinner? Or that she washes and dries three loads of laundry while he watches TV?

Leisure must be the prerogative of both sexes.

Holidays

> *"'Sometimes nowadays I hear folks
> complainin' o' bein' overtaxed with all the
> Christmas work they have do.'
> 'Well, others think that it makes a lovely
> chance for all that really enjoys givin'. . . .'"*
> Sarah Orne Jewett, "Aunt Cynthy Dallett"

*L*et's plan now for holidays that become "lovely chances" rather than overtaxing burdens. It's too easy to let the quest for perfect presents, decorations, menus, and homes make us perfectly miserable before, during, and after the *holy days*.

But we can examine our family holiday rituals. Does Santa really need three different kinds of decorated cookies when the youngest child in the house is twenty-five? Perhaps we're ready to abandon some traditions and make some new ones—enjoying the festive, celebratory atmosphere of buildings and homes decorated by others, relaxing in the leisure of days off work, being stimulated by the changes in ordinary routine, and using the holidays to spend time with those we love—guilt-free.

> *I will find peace during the holidays and extend
> it to others.*

Power

"One of the hardest things for the female psyche to bear about the use of power . . . is that it can contain in itself the seed of others' fear."

Naomi Wolf, *Fire with Fire*

If Naomi Wolf is correct, then we women of power can do something about the way we obtain power and the way we use it to neutralize the fear of others. Sometimes when we attain positions of authority, we find ourselves surrounded by the same men who have made the decisions all along. When that happens we have to be careful not to be prevented from carrying through with the differences in the female use of power. Women bring a different sensitivity to issues, a different approach, a different style. We are more inclined to share power, making it consensual and cooperative. We are more interested in mediation and resolution than in winning or losing.

I believe I can be respected without being feared.

Reality

"The winds, the sea, and the moving tides are what they are."

Rachel Carson, acceptance speech,
National Book Awards, 1952

There's much to be said for accepting what is, especially those things that can never be different—past events, human nature, mortality. When we wrap our minds around reality, we do not become discouraged or depressed; to the contrary, we find such acceptance liberating and powerful. As Margery Williams writes in *The Velveteen Rabbit*, "When you are Real, you don't mind being hurt." We accept our own reality, not the fantasy us, not the women we plan to be someday, but the women we are right now, sitting here, ten pounds overweight, feeling a little bitchy this morning, behind on some chores, at cross-purposes with someone we love. That's the reality. Having accepted it, now if we want to do something about it, we can.

The moon is. The earth is. The oak tree outside my window is. I am.

Determination

> *"Always I am determined to overcome*
> *adversity, determined to win, determined to be*
> *me, myself at my best, always female, always*
> *black, and everlastingly free."*
>
> Margaret Walker,
> "On Being Female, Black, and Free"

A determined woman is formidable indeed. She stands with feet planted firmly, sturdy legs supporting her body, chest out, shoulders back, chin up, with a firm mouth and eyes unafraid to meet the eyes of anyone else. She is determined—determined to do right by herself and her family and friends, determined to correct wrongs, determined to take responsibility for herself, determined to do what she can with what she has, no matter what the situation.

Some of us have come a long way in determination since we were younger. Dependent, passive, sweetly subservient then, we could not have dreamed of the willful, passionate women we've become. We're happy with the way we've grown and matured, happy to stand up for ourselves.

Determination, thy name is woman.

Relationships

> *"One realizes that human relationships . . .*
> *can never be wholly satisfactory, that every*
> *ego is half the time greedily seeking them,*
> *and half the time pulling away from them."*
>
> Willa Cather,
> "The Stories of Katherine Mansfield"

When relationships flounder as they inevitably do, it helps to remember that we carry within us at all times the contrarieties of wanting to be in relationships and wanting to be out of them, wanting companionship and wanting solitude, wanting affinity and wanting isolation.

When we acknowledge this truth, we can understand how elastic relationships must be, how they must be able to expand to contain these contrary moods and impulses. We may find lunching with a friend four Tuesdays in a row utterly delightful—and on the fifth Tuesday, utterly impossible. We haven't changed; the relationship hasn't changed; our needs for affinity are simply different on that fifth Tuesday. Good relationships adapt to the emotional climate of those involved.

My relationships do not always have to be
intense to be rich and nourishing.

Energy

*"Since I was sixty I've written more and had
better energy and more energy than I ever had
in my life."*

Meridel Le Sueur,
"Rites of Ancient Ripening"

One of the things that seems to give us more zip right now is other women. Whenever we attend all-women functions, we stand amazed as the energy gathers, charging the group with excitement as each contributes her energy and draws energy from the whole. Perhaps with people we trust we drop the barriers that normally keep our energy contained. Perhaps energy just multiplies exponentially. When I write with my writing groups, our collected energy gets me so high, I feel I could write an epic. Sometimes a telephone call from a single friend is enough to restore our flagging spirits as transferred energy zips over the fiber optic cables, transforming us.

*Alone I dissipate energy; with someone I can
generate it.*

Setting Limits

"Every time I say yes when I mean no, I am abandoning myself, and I end up feeling used or resentful or frantic."

Anne Lamott, *Operating Instructions*

lthough we know we must set limits for our health, sometimes we find it difficult. But the image of woman as a boundless resource of unconditional love, comfort, and nurture, perpetually awake, perpetually available, is mythical. We're real women—with limited energies and resources. To make the best use of what we have, we must set limits. We must shout our "no's" so no one can misunderstand.

Will we work unpaid overtime again this week as we did last week? NO! Will we accept another term as chairperson when we had no support from the parent organization the last time we served? NO! Will we trade our comfortable car for our daughter's severely in-need-of-repairs jalopy? NO! We will not transgress our limits again.

Setting limits does not limit me; it frees me.

Selfishness/Selflessness

> "God: 'This one is perfect. She has just
> enough selfishness.'
> The angel gasps, 'Selfishness? Is that a
> virtue?'"
>
> Erma Bombeck,
> *Houston Chronicle*, 1 May 1996

*I*n this, one of my favorite Erma Bombeck columns, God surprises an angel by choosing, as the perfect mother for a disabled child, one with "just enough selfishness." Why? Only someone who cares enough for herself to take care of herself will have the reserves to care for the child. Only a "selfish" mother will be dispassionate and objective enough to balance the needs of the child against the needs of the family. Only a "selfish" mother can weigh the needs of the child for support and nurture against the needs of the child to develop independence and self-reliance. Thank you, Erma, for reminding all of us that selfishness can be a virtue.

*Sometimes I must be selfish before I can be
selfless.*

Living in Community

> *"We have forgotten that we live outward from*
> *the center of a circle and that what is nearest*
> *to the center is most real to us."*
>
> Rebecca West, "The Meaning of Treason"

 $\mathcal{W}$e all belong to communities— communities of blood, geography, race, interests, age, nationality, recovery, religion. We can call on those communities when we are in need. When we live in community, we know that even if we choose to dwell alone, we need not be lonely.

Living in community gives us a broader perspective; when we know that others have suffered as we suffer, failed as we fail, and triumphed as we triumph, we feel camaraderie and hope. If other community members have experienced what we experience and survived, so can we. We are neither so alone nor so different nor so terrible as we thought. Giving up our uniqueness, while sometimes painful, brings relief.

> *I am an individual and I am a member of a*
> *community. Thank Goddess.*

Tidiness

"Louisa had almost the enthusiasm of an
artist over the mere order and cleanliness of
her solitary home. . . . She gloated gently
over her orderly bureau-drawers. . . ."

Mary E. Wilkins Freeman,
"A New England Nun"

Tidiness can become an obsession.
How uncomfortable to be in the
home of someone who whisks away a coffee mug before
we've finished the last sip or vacuums the dining room car-
pet while the guests are still chatting in the family room.
An inability to live with disorder for even a few minutes is
compulsive and unhealthy. Tidiness implies we're through,
we're finished, it's all over. That's seldom the case. When
I'm in the middle of a writing project, books are everywhere, spilling off the love seat, falling off the shelves,
being used as bookmarks in other books. They stay that
way until I'm finished, then I tidy up.

*Life leaves lots of raw edges and strings
sticking out—so can I.*

Destiny

"'We are all slaves to our destinies,
Concepcion. Destiny is the cage each
woman is born with.'"

Alicia Gaspar de Alba, "Cimarrona"

*H*as being destined to be women
enslaved or caged us? Earlier in our
lives we may have thought so; perhaps even now, in times
of bitterness or depression, we may think so, but ultimately
we know better. We know we can reach for an existence
above and beyond that which would seem to have been destined for us. Seldom today is anything fixed and irrevocable. What we do have to accept is our own interior
authenticity; then we use that knowledge to achieve an outer
life that matches, modifying and changing our environments and situations as we can.

*Destiny is not my cage but my container—a
container I choose for myself.*

Tolerance

*"Toleration . . . is the greatest gift of the
mind; it requires the same effort of the brain
that it takes to balance oneself on a bicycle."*
Helen Keller, *The Story of My Life*

*T*olerance is balance, walking the middle line, and compromise; tolerance is both/and instead of either/or; tolerance sees gray more often than black and white. Tolerance, like the ability to live with paradox, is a quality of maturity, yet even now it's often hard to achieve without some struggle. Sometimes it's hard to avoid thinking that what we see as good for us isn't necessarily good for everyone. Yet, we know that we must give up trying to control other people.

We don't confuse tolerance with passivity or indifference. Tolerance does not mind other people drinking when she doesn't; indifference ignores the drunken guest heading for the parking lot jingling car keys. Tolerance permits different political opinions; passivity doesn't vote.

I am tolerant, yes; indifferent, no.

Creativity

"Creativity is a shapechanger. One moment it takes this form, the next that. . . ."
Clarissa Pinkola Estés,
Women Who Run with the Wolves

*W*hen we draw from our creativity, the center of our emotion and imagination, life takes on another dimension in which the inner life dictates the outer existence. Exercising our creativity clears confusion by giving us a way to express our personal voices and allowing us to focus our energies.

Infinite are the shapes of creativity—painting landscapes, throwing pots, composing ballads, choreographing ballets, writing poetry, inventing recipes, arranging flowers, hanging artwork. We know how to evoke our creativity. We know how to relax and enjoy the process rather than concentrating on the finished product. When one creative project seems stuck, we know to switch to another one—when writing goes poorly, we plan a kitchen herb garden. We know how to allow ourselves time to do what we love.

I express my individuality through my creativity.

Intelligence

"It would be a grand dream to contribute to the sum of human knowledge, but it would be almost as satisfying to have one's original idea, however modest, put to use in the world."

Judith Chernaik,
"Honor Thy Father and Thy Mother"

ntelligence, used properly, doesn't dazzle others; it illuminates. Intelligence should be "put to use in the world." With our innate tendency toward teaching and cooperation, women can do this naturally. Women have shared their intelligence through the ages from using plants to make colorful dyes to rotating crops for increased agricultural production. And women have shared their good ideas; Emily Bissell invented the concept of selling Christmas seals to fight tuberculosis, Caresse Crosby invented the brassiere, Elizabeth Kingsley invented the double-crostic puzzle. We midlife women have plenty of time left to put our ideas to work in the world; a recent study showed that men experience brain shrinkage as they age while women do not.

I'm happy to put my intelligence to work.

Music

> *"I believe that music . . . can build a unity in*
> *women that no political rhetoric can duplicate."*
> Kay Gardner, quoted in Carol P. Christ,
> *Diving Deep and Surfacing*

*E*ven if we don't consider ourselves vocalists or musicians, we feel a rapport and kinship with others when we sing and make music together. Music loosens our adult rigidity and releases our emotions.

As adolescents we probably sat for hours in our girlfriends' bedrooms, playing records and listening to live music broadcast from distant cities. Listening to favorite music still lightens us when we feel discouraged or depressed. We set the mood for romance and social activities with background music.

Music provides solitary pleasure also, whether we turn on some rock and roll and work up a sweat dancing by ourselves or listening to a live symphony performance, smiling, shivering, and weeping as the music soars and diminishes.

> *Music is one of the inexpensive pleasures of life,*
> *an excellent form of self-therapy.*

Growth

> "Change and growth are no disgrace. To live
> long means nothing unless you are open and
> filled with love."
>
> Denise Chávez, *Face of an Angel*

*A*t our age, we're still growing, taking risks, accepting challenges, and pushing ourselves in new directions. We're more willing to grow now because we're more aware that our actions do not affect other people as much as we used to think they did; we realize we risk only ourselves. We've finished some phases of our lives, and we're ready to consider other roads. We're free at last to be who we want to be, who we have felt ourselves becoming through the past decades. We're giving up our lives as caterpillars, breaking free from chrysalides, and becoming splendid butterflies, brilliant wings trembling in the sweet breeze.

Every age has its developmental tasks. I accept the challenges of growth.

Culture Shock

"She is not at home in this world."
Katherine Anne Porter, "Flowering Judas"

We've experienced the disorientation of travel, the feeling of not belonging. We've felt it sitting on wooden benches in an electric train running through the Russian countryside, watching fellow travelers snacking on fistfuls of dried fish. We've felt it watching a wedding party process down a cobblestone street in a French village as church bells ring and people applaud from balconies. These people have different customs, speak different languages, follow different rhythms of working and playing, sleeping and eating. We're not in Kansas anymore. And isn't that nice?

Culture shock, the feeling of not belonging and temporary bewilderment, broadens our minds and hearts, teaching us to adapt to the unfamiliar, to modify our ways to the ways of others. And as we do, we begin to feel "at home" in these worlds; we find we are more flexible than we thought.

I'd like to be "at home" wherever I travel.

Transformation

> *"Without a belief in the capacity for*
> *transformation, one can become ossified."*
>
> Toni Cade Bambara,
> "What It Is I Think I'm Doing Anyhow"

*A*n essential quality of our humanity is the ability to allow ourselves to be changed. As the food we absorb is transformed by our body into energy, bones, and blood, so our life experiences transform our spirits and minds. We don't let life "have its way" with us—we're too independent and sturdy for that. But we have the capacity for change, and we can allow change to work its transformation on us. We refuse to remain stuck in the same place like a mouse in a glue trap. We refuse to believe we will never learn. We refuse to accept we can never change.

> *I accept transformation: I can hardly wait to*
> *see what I'm becoming.*

Intuition

"But still, the other voice, the intuitive,
returns, like grass forcing its way through
concrete."

Susan Griffin, "Thoughts on Writing"

*W*hen logic tells us to despair, to give up and quit because there is no way we're going to finish the project in time, be able to take the holiday we planned, or reconcile that stubborn family quarrel, fortunately we have another voice to consult. Setting aside our reason, we can listen to our intuition. What does our soul say on that subject? How does our heart respond? How does our belly react when our head makes a decision?

In middle age, we begin to trust intuition more often, accept its standards, its wishes, and its timetable. We can model using our intuition to guide others. After the charts and graphs and overheads have been put away, we can suggest that the board or the committee sit silently for a few minutes before making a decision.

My intuition can be my salvation.

Control

> *"I believe we all need to be dizzy and out of*
> *control at times, by choice or not. I like it*
> *better, of course, when I can have some*
> *control over my being out of control."*
>
> Rita Justice, *Alive and Well*

*Y*es, it's great to be out of control, and yes, I'd like to be in charge of my being out of control. How well that paradox captures our feelings. We'd rather choose riding a roller coaster than being strapped in an airplane seat during a turbulent flight, yet the dizzying plunges that leave the stomach hovering some feet above the head are similar. And all we can do in either situation is relax, say a prayer, and enjoy the ride. When unplanned events knock us off our feet, sometimes it's OK to struggle to regain control, and sometimes it's better to relax and go with the flow.

> *If I try to control the waves, I'll never learn to*
> *swim. If I submit to them, I'll float.*

Winter

"O thought I! what a beautiful thing God has made winter to be by stripping the trees and letting us see their shapes and forms."
Dorothy Wordsworth, *Grasmere Journals*

*E*ven though we no longer live by the cycle of daylight and dark, something about the shorter days and longer nights of winter encourages even city-dwellers to relax, settle in, go to bed earlier, cocoon in our houses. Our bodies and spirits long for such restful quiet.

We are not depressed by the darkness of winter because we know it is prefatory—under the snowdrifts lies a green promise, in the ashes glow the sparks to rekindle another fire, in the stillness of our spirits our creativity quickens.

Winter provides a model of quiet waiting and trust; we experience the light only by cycling through the dark. We cannot always be in full bloom; sometimes we must concentrate on the growth of the roots, the hidden strength underneath the blooms.

I will not hurry spring; winter's quiet blesses me, too.

Endurance

*"What she bequeathed me unwittingly,
ironically, was fortitude—the fortitude of
those who have had to live under the blow."*
Hortense Calisher, "The Middle Drawer"

A gift of suffering is fortitude. As the clay vessel fired under extreme heat becomes a vase, as the athlete trains through pain to expand her physical limits, as childish innocence is tempered to wisdom by contact with the world, so those who suffer learn endurance. Even though suffering can have positive effects, we do not ignore it. We still do our best to ameliorate or eradicate it, whether it has been inflicted on us or someone else, but when that is impossible, we learn to become stronger under it.

After suffering, endurance says, "I'm still here."

Distractions

> *"She is known to be brisk and absentminded.*
> *She is known for her look of perpetual*
> *distraction."*
>
> Kirsten Backstrom, "Swamp"

*D*istraction seems to be an inherent element of women's lives. The minutiae of daily living threaten to overwhelm us, sweeping us away from our soul work. Sometimes we feel like kindergarten teachers toward the end of the morning with twenty or more small voices making demands; "Teacher, tie my shoes." "I spilled my paint." "I need a tissue." "Teacher, Billy took my truck." "I want to go home now." "I have to go potty." What we want to do is sit them down in a circle and read them a charming little fable.

We're learning to let some desires and demands, no matter how worthy, wait. We're learning to say no, not now. We're learning not to be pleased that so many people want us for so many different things.

> *Distractions can't sweep me off my feet if I*
> *don't let them.*

Wholeness

*"Seeking the numinous in life's second half
we look to what heals, makes whole,
we turn in
where divinity quickens the self at last."*

Sally Ridgway, "Prickly Magic—A Found
Poem for Jean Shinoda Bolen"

We strive for wholeness, wanting to bring together all of our roles—mothers, wives, companions, lovers, friends, daughters, workers, writers, radicals, healers, guides—into one cohesive whole. We don't want to compartmentalize or fragment our lives into the parts we play. As daughters, we also mother. As writers, we also love. As colleagues, we also befriend.

We also seek to accept and integrate all the separate personalities we contain within ourselves—shy preteen, rebellious adolescent, flirtatious coed, angry writer, sexy partner, independent worker, passive committee person, and nonconforming spiritual disciple. With integration comes healing.

I contain divisiveness, but I am whole.

Having a Sense of Wonder

> *"In her face I saw a quality of wonder, the*
> *quality of a child searching for a fairy tale."*
> Paula María Espinosa, "Three Day Flight"

*W*e don't ever want to be so grown up that we can't thrill to the unexpected and the wonderful in our world. The heroism of a cat who walks through flames to carry her kittens to safety. The desire and achievement of the son of migrant workers who, despite never having had more than three consecutive months of schooling before high school, earns admission to West Point. The devotion of a spouse caring for a partner with a chronic disease. The silver sounds of a children's choir. A pair of golden-feathered geese nesting on a frozen pond. A young man bursting into tears of joy on his wedding day. Moonrise on the desert. A miniature waterfall cascading into a basin of ferns.

> *May I always be able to say "how wonderful"*
> *and mean it.*

Postholiday Depression

> *"As she said every year after they had all
> gone, Christmas was a duty as much as
> anything."*
>
> Leslie Thomas, "The Surprise Package"

When holidays become duties rather than pleasure, when our holiday expectations have not been met, we may feel miserable afterward. But we know what we can do to prevent postholiday depression. We can refuse to participate in holiday activities that do not hold real meaning for us. If we think exchanging greeting cards with people we see every day is ridiculous, then we won't. If we don't see the point in exhausting ourselves decorating when we're spending most of the holidays out of town, then we won't decorate.

And after the holidays have passed, if bitterness still lingers, we can replenish our bodies by exercising and eating nutritious food, we can refresh our spirits in ways appropriate for us, and we can analyze what went wrong and do our best to eliminate those factors in the next holiday.

Depression need not follow a holiday.

Accepting Paradox

"All of the deepest paradoxes are not opposed at all but are clearly one, two sides of a single understanding."

Alix Kates Shulman, *Drinking the Rain*

$\mathcal{C}$oming to terms with age helps us come to terms with paradox. Many aspects of aging are paradoxical; as we grow older in time, we grow younger in spirit. We find that limits provide choices rather than barriers, and that centering and focusing make us more expansive. So we understand the deep truth behind such paradoxes as: "There is movement in nonmovement." "Nothing has changed and everything has changed." "The only way to follow a path is to leave it." "I can succeed in failure." "There is health in illness." Yes, we can laugh and weep simultaneously. Yes, we can spend a rich day doing nothing. Yes, sometimes we are never so alive as when in the presence of death.

Living in paradox is nothing new to me.

Wildness

> *"The garden with the fountains was man-made*
> *and docile and friendly, . . . but the hills were*
> *wild and separate from man, enemies! . . ."*
>
> Naomi Mitchison,
> "The Poor Relation and the Secretary"

ometimes we have to leave the gardens and the fountains and head for the wild hills. Wildness was once part of our women's landscape, and something within us responds to a call to wildness. We feel a need to check ourselves out and see if we still have it; we have to take some risks. We have to test our limits— physical, emotional, spiritual, and intellectual. Sometimes we just have to relinquish the safety net of jobs, partners, and relationships and venture the high wire alone, balancing by ourselves.

> *The nature of the wildness I seek doesn't*
> *matter; occasionally pushing myself beyond my*
> *safe limits does.*

Education

"The largest numbers of women returning to school are those under thirty-five and over fifty-five."

Jane Porcino, *Growing Older, Getting Better*

Good for us who return to school—to learn or relearn skills we need to make a living, to satisfy our intellectual interests, and to gain self-fulfillment. We better our own lives and enhance the lives of all those with whom we come in contact.

When we return to college at midlife, we find our worldly knowledge puts us far ahead of younger peers. After all, skills such as writing and painting can be taught, but the habits of reflection and observation with which we study and write cannot. We bring perspectives to classrooms that enrich discussion for everyone.

Learning is living; I will be a student and be alive.

Addictions

> "I can become addicted to almost anything if I set my mind to it."
>
> Anonymous

*A*ddiction does require our participation. There are life conditions so conflict-ridden and confining that we turn to drugs, alcohol, food, or shopping for temporary freedom from our misery. But we find that our rebellion is also our punishment. Using an addiction as a substitute for expressing our feelings eventually causes us to lose the ability to feel.

Midlife is a good time to examine our addictions and choose not to continue any pattern of behavior injurious to ourselves or others. We can choose to become addicted to being healthy, to expressing our feelings appropriately, to loving ourselves. It's never too late.

I can set my mind to freeing myself from my addictions.

Endings

"Nothing begins when it begins and nothing's over when it's over."

Margaret Atwood, *The Robber Bride*

I don't want to write "the end" after this meditation because it isn't the end. Perhaps you started reading the book in March or September, and you have many more months to go. Or perhaps you did start reading January 1, and you've read a meditation every day—but tomorrow you plan to start again.

There is nothing ever final about the end of anything—not this book, not a job, not a relationship, not a political era, not a century, not even a millennium. We remember the motto of Mary Stuart, Queen of Scots; "In my end is my beginning." An ending, like a beginning, turns out to be just another passage, a threshold, a space between something known and something else unknown.

In my life, I will cherish all the endings that never come to an end.

Selected Bibliography

While I worked on this book, I read only works by women, adding to the appreciation I already had for women writers from more than twenty years as a college English teacher. To give full credit to these authors for their wisdom and inspiration, I've also listed the titles of their works. Many of the works quoted may be found in the following anthologies:

Barnstone, Aliki, and Willis Barnstone, eds. *A Book of Women Poets from Antiquity to Now*. Rev. ed. NY: Schocken, 1992.

Berman, Phillip L., ed. *The Courage to Grow Old*. NY: Ballantine, 1989.

Cahill, Susan, ed. *Writing Women's Lives*. NY: Harper, 1994.

Cole, Thomas R., and Mary G. Winkler, eds. *The Oxford Book of Aging*. Oxford: Oxford UP, 1994.

Ferguson, Mary Anne. *Images of Women in Literature*. 4th ed. Boston: Houghton, 1986.

Fernández, Roberta, ed. *In Other Words: Literature by Latinas of the United States.* Houston: Arte Público, 1994.

Gilbert, Sandra, and Susan Gubar. *The Norton Anthology of Literature by Women.* NY: Norton, 1985.

Martz, Sandra Haldeman, ed. *I Am Becoming the Woman I've Wanted.* Watsonville, CA: Papier-Mache, 1994.

Martz, Sandra Haldeman, ed. *If I Had My Life to Live Over I Would Pick More Daisies.* Watsonville, CA: Papier-Mache, 1992.

Park, Christine, and Caroline Heaton, eds. *Close Company: Stories of Mothers and Daughters.* NY: Ticknor, 1989.

Sennet, Dorothy, with Anne Czarniecki. *Vital Signs: International Stories on Aging.* St. Paul: Graywolf, 1991.

Spender, Dale, and Janet Todd. *British Women Writers.* NY: Bedrick, 1989.

Sternburg, Janet. *The Writer on Her Work.* NY: Norton, 1988.

Washington, Mary Helen, ed. *Black-Eyed Susans/Midnight Birds.* NY: Anchor, 1990.

Zahava, Irene, ed. *My Mother's Daughter.* Freedom, CA: Crossing, 1991.

Index

About the Author

SuzAnne C. Cole, fifty-five, is a writer and an adjunct instructor of English for the Houston Community College System in Houston, Texas. Married for thirty-three years, she and her husband have three adult sons and two daughters-in-law.

Since turning fifty, SuzAnne has found herself happier than at any other time in her life. This book, the result of reading, journaling, writing for publication, and involvement in personal growth work and women's support groups, shares her contentment in the form of daily meditations.